FUN and SAFETY on TWO WHEELS

FUN and SAFETY on TWO WHEELS:

Bicycles
Mopeds
Scooters
Motorcycles

by Charles Yerkow

G.P. Putnam's Sons · New York

All photographs are by Charles Yerkow
with the exception of the following:
   American Jawa Ltd., pages 130, 133
   Butler & Smith, Inc., pages 20, 42, 107, 121
   Sam Curchack, pages 72, 94, 104
   Don Whyte, page 129
   Shimano American Corp., page 39

Copyright © 1979 by Charles Yerkow
All rights reserved. Published
simultaneously in Canada by
Longman Canada Limited, Toronto.
PRINTED IN THE UNITED STATES OF AMERICA

Library of Congress Cataloging in Publication Data
Yerkow, Charles
   Fun and safety on two wheels.
   Includes index.
   SUMMARY: Advice for the cyclist on using a bicycle,
moped, scooter, or motorcycle both enjoyably and safely.
   1. Cycling—Juvenile literature. 2. Motorcycling—
Juvenile literature. [1. Bicycles and bicycling.
2. Mopeds. 3. Motorcycling. 4. Motor scooters]
I. Title.
GV1043.5.Y47   796.6   78-32137
ISBN 0-399-20687-6

Contents

1 Get Started Right 9
2 Don't Ride a Neglected Machine 31
3 Know Your Engine 55
4 You—the Rider 79
5 Your Survival in Traffic 97
6 Long-Distance Touring 117
7 Rough Riding and Racing 127
Index 137

Acknowledgments

For providing me with valuable technical information and the necessary material during the writing and photographic work for this book, I extend my sincere thanks and appreciation to Z. Sevcik, J. Tucik, J. Tamasi, K. Bojer, R. Hansen and J. Mendlovsky of American Jawa Ltd.; to Luciano Cortese of Portofino Moped and Bicycle International (importers of the Pacer line of mopeds); to Richard Kahn of Butler & Smith, Inc. (importers of BMW motorcycles); and to Yoshizo Shimano of Shimano American Corporation (manufacturers of quality components for bicycles).

My special thanks also to Don Whyte, Whitey Elligash, Susan and Ed Kaeding, and Sam Curchack for their cooperation and assistance.

To Lila Perl

Get Started Right

1

About a year ago a teenager glowed with pride and happiness when his father gave him a brand-new bicycle for his fifteenth birthday. It was a lightweight 10-speed model, a white frame, gleaming chrome, reflective tires, headlight and reflectors, and the fabulous disc brake on the rear wheel.

The disc brake, something new to the boy, was an invitation to get on and ride—and check out its stopping ability. He had occasionally used a friend's 10-speeder, and he knew how to handle the shifting mechanism; but the disc brake was something new.

First, however, was the job of oiling and polishing up every part of the elegant-looking machine, including the spokes, rims, and everything else that gleamed. Then the boy raced down his driveway, across the road, and slammed into a stone wall. He died of head injuries.

He was considered a careful rider. He had been on bikes most of his life. The machine was equipped with efficient caliper brakes on the front wheel and the highly effective disc brake on the rear wheel. There was no car on the road at the time it happened, and both the road and the driveway were dry. Why didn't he use the brakes? Why did he lose control? What happened?

He did use the brakes, but the brakes didn't work. The boy had oiled them. The front caliper pads couldn't hold against the oiled wheel rim, and the rear disc pads couldn't hold against the oiled disc.

This unfortunate accident tells you two facts: Never ride any machine until you've tried the brakes the moment you start rolling. And never ride a brand-new machine until after you've read every page of your *owner's handbook*. Had the boy read his instructions, he would be alive today because he would have learned at once that you NEVER put oil on these parts of a brake system (and that goes for motorcycles, too).

Every year about 30,000 bicycle riders are killed, most of them because somebody ignored some basic factor regarding safety.

Whether you're an old hand at riding two-wheelers or a beginner, this book will help you better understand your machine—whether it's a bicycle, a moped, a scooter, or a full motorcycle. It also should help you develop the proper attitude for safe riding in traffic and on open roads. The key word is *safety,* but it goes beyond the simple routine of "be careful and obey traffic signs."

Real safety starts with how much you really know about your two-wheeler and with your personal outlook on using a two-wheeler. All experts agree that your first half hour spent with a rider of a machine will either make you into someone to be admired or break you into someone who rides stupidly.

For example, if you don't know why one of your wheels is wobbling, then you don't know much about the simple technical side of axles, hubs, and bolts. And that means you're riding a dangerous machine. If you can't figure out why the engine on your moped or motorcycle is sluggish and does not always respond to the throttle, then you either don't know your carb or are neglecting it—and riding a dangerous machine.

A friend of mine was on his motorcycle on the shoulder of a highway, waiting for a flock of speeding cars to pass so that he could make a U-turn (which was illegal). When the traffic thinned and he thought it safe to shoot across, he shifted into low, gunned the engine, and started to cross. He thought he had plenty of space, but as he got nearly halfway across, his engine konked out. In a frenzy he tried to foot-push himself back to the safety of the shoulder, but a car bearing down on him struck him broadside. The impact hurled him and the machine eighty feet down the highway, totally demolishing the machine and killing him. He didn't have a chance with that unreliable engine.

Highway accident statistics offer shocking figures, often divided into categories, telling you at what sort of location accidents took place, day or night, fatal or not, wet or dry surface, and so on. From such statistics a lot of theories, rules and laws have been worked out. They tell us all what to watch out for in traffic and how to conduct ourselves at corners and intersections. In no uncertain terms their message is to obey all traffic control signs and lights.

Besides all this designed for your safety, the manufacturer tries to give you the utmost in protection where the vehicle itself is concerned. In the case of automobiles, manufacturers take care to eliminate protruding knobs and sharp edges inside the car, designing steering wheels so they'll collapse on impact, providing belts and air bags, and offering power steering and power brakes for ease of operation. In the case of two-wheelers, manufacturers give you the best in all-around construction, dependable braking systems, and effective operating controls.

All these things physically protect (to a degree) auto drivers and riders of two-wheelers when there is an accident. But does it spell *safety?* A reliable vehicle is one thing, but true protection and safety are something else. It all narrows down to one principle: *The vehicle operator's familiarity with his machine and his attitude about controlling that machine in traffic are what really spell safety.*

Imagine any kind of street or highway accident, and see if you can uncover the real causes that led to it, the way a professional investigator would. You'll need answers to a lot of questions, and you'll have to examine the vehicles in question and the location where the accident took place. Even in such an imagined case you'll begin to understand the *controlling factors* and the *contributing circumstances*. These will help later to keep you out of trouble.

Newspaper stories say that "the car driver lost control" or that the accident was "due to mechanical failure" or that "poor visibility, rain, snow, fog" was the real culprit. Such stories will at least make you aware that anything can happen at any time because danger lurks everywhere. As a rider of a two-wheeler, what exactly will protect you from all the dangerous situations when you're out there tooling around?

A simple, highly effective answer is given by experts who have actually handled all sorts of motorized vehicles under all sorts of imaginable conditions and who have devoted a lot of time to the special problem of road safety. Their main point is that only two things cause accidents (and I agree totally because my own research in this area has uncovered the same two points). One cause is the unexpected mechanical failure of some part of the machine (car or two-wheeler). The other cause is the unexpected behavior of the vehicle operator, which, of course, includes careless behavior.

Mechanical failure could be caused by anything, of course. But most often it can be blamed on the fact the owner neglected his periodic maintenance. That means his machine was not in good working condition; he neglected to inspect certain important parts, and therefore, those parts were out of adjustment and contributed to the problem.

An operator's behavior could be caused by anything, too, but most often it can be traced to lack of training to cope with traffic situations and lack of awareness, or indifference, to such situations.

If you knew that the brake cable on your two-wheeler was frayed and might snap apart at any moment, you would be careful indeed not to ride too fast in crowded places because you'd be *expecting* a stopping problem. If someone told you that a couple of cars in the tight curve up ahead had smashed together against the divider, you would slow down and approach that curve carefully because you'd be *expecting* something out of the ordinary.

You're expected to handle the unexpected. But how can you handle it when you've never been taught how to look for it? Pilots of aircraft, during their flight test, must demonstrate to the examiner that they can handle the unexpected. However, drivers of automobiles and riders of two-wheelers are not asked to demonstrate any special skills or prove that they understand the mechanical side of their machines.

Learning about accidents through personal experience can be an uncomfortably costly way. So let's start at the absolute beginning, before you even straddle the two-wheeler of your choice. Later you'll advance to the business of getting to know yourself as far as your riding is concerned and also of knowing about the key points of controlling two-wheelers. We'll discuss two-wheelers (bicycles, mopeds, scooters, motorcycles) intended for street and road use, long-distance touring, and even rough riding.

DRESS FOR RIDING

Go to a motocross or scramble or high-speed road race, and see what the competitors are wearing: leather pants and jacket, boots, gloves, helmet and face shield, or goggles. Not because they want to look tough and not because they want to sweat under all that clothing. What they want is head and body protection in case they spill or crash.

A bicycle rider would be smart to wear gloves (even in the summer) every time he goes for a spin and to wear full shoes instead of going barefooted or in open-toed sandals. Skinned knuckles and broken toes are painful and show you up as a rider with very little experience. Motorized machines and higher speeds demand that you protect your head and body, including hands and feet.

Dress to suit the circumstances. One rider went out one winter day on his motorcycle but forgot to take along his gloves. Soon his hands got so cold that he was forced to tuck his left hand under his thigh to warm it. Then, when his wheels hit a rut and with only one hand on the handlebar, he lost control momentarily and went careening off the road. He wasn't hurt; but his tank was dented badly, and the front fork didn't face the right direction. He no longer forgets his gloves.

Even if you're riding a moped or a scooter, it pays to wear a helmet and eye protection of some sort. Also, wear clothing that's visible—bright colors or some reflective material taped around your jacket and sleeves and even on the helmet (white helmets are more visible than dark ones).

Even when riding a bicycle or moped, protect yourself by wearing full shoes and gloves. On a Class B moped, scooter, or motorcycle, wear an approved helmet with eye shield or goggles and be sure your feet can reach the ground.

Your next step is to become familiar with your particular two-wheeler.

YOUR OWNER'S HANDBOOK
For some reason this seems to be the most ignored piece of informative literature. A lot of people who spend hard-earned money on a great machine should want to know in detail how the

machine is put together, how it should be handled, and how it should be serviced. But they ignore the handbook and seem to think such information is stored in their minds and will be available automatically whenever they need it. How wrong they are!

The more you know about your two-wheeler, the safer you'll be while riding it. And if you have a breakdown on the road, you'll at least know where to start looking and what you can and cannot do about it.

This book could not possibly explain everything about every particular bicycle, moped, scooter, or motorcycle. The particular details of your machine are to be found in your owner's handbook. For example, the removal of something will differ from machine to machine, but in all cases that "something" is removable. Similarly, the connecting of one part to another will differ from machine to machine, but in all cases that "something" is connectable.

Make it a point to dig out your owner's handbook every once in a while, along with the parts list, and reacquaint yourself with your two-wheeler. You'll be surprised what you'll learn. That information, plus the material you'll find in this book, will put you far ahead of the crowd.

Since regulations about two-wheelers differ from state to state and since even your friends and your dealer may not have the up-to-date information, go to your local Department of Motor Vehicles and get the latest copy of the requirements. It's your only insurance that you're a legal rider. Also, be sure to check on the law regarding your *financial responsibility* requirements.

SIZE ALWAYS COUNTS

There's a saying that a machine must fit the rider and the rider must fit the machine. Old-timers know the value of this saying because a long time ago they learned how uncomfortable it is to ride a two-wheeler which is either too small or too big. For example, if you can't reach the ground with your feet from the seat of a moped, scooter, or motorcycle, you could find yourself in trouble, and if you can't squeeze the hand brake and clutch levers, you're in bigger trouble.

Where a bicycle is concerned, straddle the top bar, and check the clearance under your crotch. If you don't have at least one inch, you're on a frame that's too big, or the wheels are too big, and this has nothing to do with how high the seat is. Once you have the right size bike, then set the seat height so your pedaling leg will be nearly straight when your foot is at the bottom of the stroke and your toes point downward. Pedal with the ball of your foot, not the arch. But be sure that at least two inches of the seat post are inside the frame tube. The nut which holds the seat post in place is right at the top of the frame tube; loosen it, set the seat up or down as needed, and then be sure to tighten the nut. Another nut under the seat lets you tilt it, for comfort.

A moped seat can be adjusted in the same way, but the seat height is set so that your feet rest on the ground when you're on the seat.

As a rule, seats on scooters and motorcycles are fixed and cannot be raised or lowered, so if you can't reach the ground with your feet (not just the toes!), start looking for another machine.

Of course, the brake levers on two-wheelers are vitally important, and you must be able to squeeze them easily to slow down or bring the machine to a stop. Yet many people buy machines which are too big, with spring-loaded levers too tough to squeeze effectively. Such riders are menaces to others and in constant danger themselves. So, before you buy that terrific-looking bike, first see how well you can wrap your fingers around the levers and whether you can squeeze with enough natural force to activate the brake or the clutch.

Where a growing youngster is involved, people often say, "He'll grow up, and then it'll be just right for him." But he'll be riding something he can't control properly, and it's his life at stake! Is a life worth that risk?

ONE BIG PROBLEM

There's one problem common to all two-wheelers, from a fine lightweight bicycle to a 900-pound touring motorcycle. They can be stolen—easily.

"Not when I wrap this chain and lock around it," you say as you

A bicycle rider must be able to straddle the top bar easily, set the seat height so the pedaling leg will be straight on the downstroke. Use the ball of the foot, not the arch.

show off the finest theft-prevention device money can buy.

Remember this: All chains, cables, lockbars, and keys, even doubled up, will serve only to make it a little harder for the crook to steal your machine. Friend Tom was in the construction business, and it was easy for him to sink a massive steel bar into the concrete floor of his garage alongside the house. Then he chained down each wheel and the frame with separate chains. Then he locked the garage door with one center and two side bolts. Then he couldn't believe his eyes when one morning he found his machine gone! With all that precaution, his $4,200 bike was stolen. Well, he got a new machine, and he has added two burglar-alarm systems to the garage setup. "You damn near have to sleep with your bike if you want to make sure it's safe from the scum!" he said.

Admittedly, Tom's case is unusual. Your worry will be when you have to leave your machine somewhere while you visit or go shopping. Since theft insurance is rather high in price for the average rider, you must depend on your own methods of theft prevention.

First, jot down for your record the serial number of your machine and every other number you can find on the frame, rear fork of a bicycle, side of the engine, and so on—just in case your two-wheeler is stolen and the police find it and you need to identify it.

Secondly, always use a chain or other device when you leave your machine for any period of time. Avoid wrapping the chain or cable around some short pole over which the thief can easily lift the bike, chain and all. Also avoid leaving your two-wheeler in dark and secluded areas where the thief can take his time and not be noticed by others.

Finally, make it a rule to take a look at the situation every few minutes—yes, every few minutes, because once a thief falls in love with your machine, he works very fast. Of course, if your machine is stolen, report the theft immediately to the police.

A SAFE START

Perhaps you're already riding a two-wheeler of some kind. You're having fun, and you want to keep it that way. Nevertheless, you owe it to yourself to know certain simple technical things because only then will you ride with a relaxed body rather than be in a state of mental and physical tension. A tense rider is not a safe rider. If you worry whether your brakes will work or the chain will slip or the machine will slide out from under you in the next curve, then you're riding with trouble.

You must understand two general areas—the technical and the

personal. The technical concerns the machine. The personal concerns you and your place in traffic.

Put one fact into your mind, and keep it there always: *Any two-wheeler will work for you, but no two-wheeler will ever THINK for you.*

BICYCLES
All bicycles have a frame, a seat, two wheels, a handlebar, a chain over some sprockets or gears, pedals, and a brake system. Some bikes have fenders and a kickstand, but these items are left off high-performance models in order to keep the weight down. Many states and communities have laws regarding safety equipment which must be on a bicycle. You must have a bell or horn, but not a whistle or siren; a white headlight and a red taillight for riding at night; reflective tires or a reflector mounted on the spokes of each wheel and also on the pedals (front and back sides); a large colorless reflector at the frame head and a red one for the rear. Stores selling bicycles must provide your machine with these items in order for you to be riding legally.

The average bicycle weighs around thirty pounds and may cost anywhere from $50 to several hundred dollars—some very special bikes cost several thousand dollars! The purpose to which you will put your bike determines the model to buy. A *single-speed coaster brake model* for general riding is not practical in hill country or for continuous fast speeds. A *3-speeder* is a good all-around model, and the *5-, 10-, and even 15-speed types* give you all the gearing you'll ever need.

When the first bicycle was "invented" in France in 1791, the front wheel was not steerable, nor did the wheels have rubber tires, yet by 1793 people were actually using these contraptions to race each other. By 1818 "improved" machines were on the market in England and in the United States and the bicycle continued in popularity, always with improvements, until it reached today's peak—well over 100 million bikes tooling around as the leading outdoor recreational activity.

MOTORCYCLES

About 100 years after the birth of the original bicycle, two German inventors, Gottlieb Daimler and Karl Benz, fitted a four-stroke engine into a massive frame with large wheels, and the first motorcycle was created. Then, in 1901, Oscar Hedstrom produced the first practical single-cylinder motorcycle in the United States. A few years later he introduced the twin four-stroker, the forerunner of the famous *Indian* line.

The general street and touring models range in weight from 200 to around 900 pounds and cost anywhere from several hundred to several thousand dollars. Most are four-strokers, but a few still use

Known all over the world as quality top performers, BMW four-stroke motorcycles feature opposed twin cylinders from 600cc to 1000cc capacity, with shaft drive. Note the front disc brake and totally enclosed engine components.

This rugged Jawa 350cc twin two-stroker is typical of general street bikes, with automatic oil injection and featuring an automatic clutch. Note the large drum brakes and the enclosed chain.

the reliable and very simple two-stroke engines. Cruising speed capabilities range from a slow 60 to more than 130 miles per hour (mph), if you want to end up with a speeding ticket.

    Most motorcycles rely on a battery and coil ignition system, but some also use a magneto for the ignition and the battery only for the electrical system, including the self-starter. All of them use a clutch and a set of from three to six forward gears.

SCOOTERS

These are the small-wheeled machines which appeared in Europe during World War II. After the war our police departments used them (and still do) for a variety of jobs. Some scooters have an automatic centrifugal clutch while others employ a regular transmission, with gear shifter and clutch lever. Some still use the small wheels; others are mounted on larger wheels and handle almost like a big motorcycle. A scooter is more economical to operate than a

Step-through designs are standard for scooters, with engine sizes from weak to powerful and features from meager to plentiful. This 125cc Tatran has an electric starter, directionals, and even a glove box!

motorcycle but not as economical as a moped. Scooters are less expensive than some motorcycles but cost more than a moped. You can still see some Italian Vespa and Lambretta models and Czechoslovakian Jawa Tatrans running around.

MOPEDS

These are unique machines indeed, a combination of a bicycle with a small economical engine mounted in the frame. *Mo*tor and *ped*als spells moped, which the law defines as "limited-use motorcycles" in basically two classes. Don't rush out and buy one until you've checked fully with your dealer and your local Department of Motor Vehicles regarding the requirements of age, licensing, insurance, the wearing of helmets, and the like.

The engine is nearly always a single cylinder two-stroke type of less than 50 cc (cubic centimeter) displacement and producing from 1 to 2 hp (horsepower). Weight is around 100 pounds, and top speed is held to 17 or 25 (miles per hour), depending on the model and state regulations. The point here is that any moped can travel 100 and more miles on 1 gallon of gasoline! Mopeds usually use the "automatic" centrifugal clutch, so that anyone who can ride a bicycle can surely ride a moped. All you have to do is start the engine, get on and open the throttle, and then know where the brakes are to come to a stop.

In almost all instances the engine is placed just in front of the pedals, but there are some variations. For example, on a very popular model the engine is mounted over the front wheel and drives the front wheel by friction. Other manufacturers produce *battery-powered* machines—no exhaust fumes, no fuel worry, no engine repairs. On these models the battery must be recharged, of course, and the operational distance is therefore limited.

SHIFTING GEARS

On a single-speed coaster brake bicycle you have no gears to shift, and you therefore ride only as fast as you're able to turn the pedals.

On the multispeed models you have a trigger, twistgrip, or levers

24 / *Fun and Safety on Two Wheels*

Portofino Pacer mopeds use a single drive chain and a starting clutch. The efficient single cylinder two-stroke Morini engine is fed by a Dell'Orto carb, while the rear swing arm and Franzoni fork provide smooth riding.

with which to select the gear you need for the riding conditions—a low gear for going uphill or against the wind, a normal gear for level riding, and a high gear for speeding. Always shift while pedaling at an easy pace, never when you're straining the chain. And never backpedal a 5- or 10-speeder and try to shift gears.

    To slow down and stop, on coaster brake models use back pressure on the pedals; on other models squeeze the hand brake levers to bring the caliper or disc pads into action.

Get Started Right / 25

After starting the engine of a moped, ride away by simply twisting the throttle to speed up the engine, at which point the centrifugal clutch automatically engages the drive gear and starts you rolling. To go faster, open the throttle more. There is usually only one gear; that means you can go only so fast and no faster. On two-gear models the shift to the next higher gear is automatic—no clutch for you to squeeze and no shift lever to move.

To slow down, shut the throttle, and then use the hand brake levers to come to a stop.

Jawa mopeds use two chains and feature a decompression lever to ease starting. Ignition is transistorized. The nicest feature of all mopeds is the 100 miles and more on one gallon of gas.

You ride a scooter and a motorcycle (after starting the engine) by first squeezing the clutch lever (disengaging) and then using your foot to tap the shift lever down into first gear. Then, as you slowly open the throttle twistgrip, you begin releasing the clutch lever at the same time, slowly, until the machine starts to pull away. You can go only so fast in any one gear; therefore, you must shift to the next gear—squeezing the clutch lever and at the same time closing the throttle so the engine won't race, shifting with your foot, and then pouring it on as you release the clutch. You repeat this until you reach top gear; some motorcycles have three gears, some four, some five, some six.

To slow down, you can do it the fun way by reversing the whole shifting pattern, using the gears to slow down (and, if you don't know how to do it, wearing out the clutch plates), or you can simply use the foot brake and the hand brake levers *together* to slow down enough to disengage the clutch and shift to neutral, then use the brakes to come to a full stop.

More handling techniques will be explained later.

As you can see, all two-wheelers are easy enough to handle and can be brought to a stop—even a panic stop—with no trouble at all. But surely you can also see that any machine not in good working condition could create a problem for a rider who needs every control to work effectively. Sometimes people have accidents through neglect of their machines, and at other times through wrong personal attitudes about riding and traffic situations.

In my first week of riding I lived through six accidents. Each was caused by some part of the machine not working the way it was expected to work (in one instance the horn not sounding!) or by the fact I took too much for granted—"I'll never be involved in an accident" attitude. After six accidents it was time to pause and take stock, and I did. Since then I have had no more accidents. Knock on wood! Experience teaches you a lot.

Experience also teaches you a lot when it comes to buying a machine, new or used.

Whether you're interested in buying a high-performance 10-speed bicycle, an inexpensive moped or scooter, or a motorcycle, the many models on the market will bewilder you. Which is the right one for you? It's risky to give advice, so let's stick to fundamentals that dictate the buying of almost any piece of machinery.

Always start out by being very curious about the place where you're shopping. Then be very cautious about deciding on any machine. Finally, take your time to check out a few other places before deciding on *the* machine for you.

Not long ago a friend of mine bought three new bikes at the local bicycle store which advertised big discounts. One was for his daughter, another for his wife, and the third for himself—his being a 10-speeder, the other two 3-speeders. When the three bicycles went out of adjustment at nearly the same time and within two weeks of purchase, my friend, who is not mechanically inclined, lugged them back to the store and asked for shift mechanism adjustments. A few days after he picked up the bikes, he and his family discovered that the shifting mechanisms were causing the same problem. This time a good mechanic adjusted the ailing bikes, but my friend doesn't speak highly of the store: "They're good at selling, but they're no help when something goes wrong.... I guess they just don't have trained mechanics."

Another friend bought a used 250 cc motorcycle. Everything was all right until he took a friend for a ride. Every time they hit a bump the rear bottomed so badly that the wheel ripped against the fender. The dealer who had sold the machine was willing to make the necessary adjustment on the rear shock absorbers—at a cost of $40! Hearing that, I showed my friend how to reposition the rear shock retaining rings (most motorcycles have them built in) with ease in ten minutes.

Both experiences are the kind you don't need. Remember, some places sell machines but will not be of much help when something goes wrong, so a "bargain" in such places can turn out to mean trouble for you.

If you already have in mind a machine and the store where you plan to buy it, pick up folders on other machines, compare features, performance, and price, and then consider how far from your home this particular store is located. How far do you want to travel when you need service and parts? If you have friends who own similar machines, talk over the problems with them—the friendliness and prompt service of the store, reliability of work, and costs. Make as many inquiries as you can about the dealer because you want to protect yourself against the "wheeler-dealer" who disappears about the time you need him.

Large merchandisers have trained technicians and repairmen, and they're definitely concerned with the customer's satisfaction. Many independent dealers also operate on this "friendliness and satisfaction" principle. Look around and select the place that pleases you. It's to your advantage to be critical. Are you impressed favorably with the place? Does the salesperson have the answers to your technical questions? Are you being hammered toward one and only one machine? Are prices posted clearly, or are you being sized up for what the traffic will bear? Can you have a look at the workshop? Is the shop orderly or does it resemble a junkyard? Can you have a demonstration ride? If there are complaining customers around, talk to them. Be curious, and don't be in a hurry.

Buying a used machine from a private seller has its special problems because you have no way of knowing what his machine went through before he decided to sell it. Can you believe the seller's reason for selling? Make a careful inspection of the tires, the shift and brakes, the seat and hand grips, the paint job. Do these show abuse? How does the engine sound and behave? How easily does the derailleur shift? Are the wheels wobbling? How does the machine feel when you ride it? And if you're not sure of your own opinion, have a mechanic inspect the machine for you.

Whether the machine is new or used, never feel that you're going to miss out on a good buy. A better deal may be waiting for you elsewhere.

Be careful about "evaluation test reports" reported occasionally in magazines devoted to two-wheelers. It is one thing for a report to state that the front fork broke when subjected to a standard test load (that would be downright bad manufacturing!). But it's quite another thing to say the machine behaved below standard at high speed in a curve on a macadam road (that would be one rider's experience). You should not accept these reports at face value and without further questioning.

Advice: Be selective in what you read, and use common sense to interpret the statements in relation to the overall purpose and intent of the machine in question.

BASIC ACCESSORIES

If you decide to add side baskets or bags or a nifty luggage rack to your machine, make sure these things are not blocking any of the reflectors and particularly not the rear stoplight. And when you load the side bags, distribute the weight evenly so that you don't end up wondering why the machine pulls to one side.

Some motorcycle riders like to outfit their machines with chromed "crashbars" which are supposed to protect the legs in case of a spill. Okay, but don't buy the type of crashbar which is attached with a flimsy metal strap and a few bolts because these are only for show rather than real protection. Some riders don't like crashbars, claiming they're dangerous in a spill because they tend to flip the machine instead of letting things slide naturally. You'll have to judge for yourself on this argument; if you buy them, get tough ones!

A word of caution about windshields on mopeds, scooters, and motorcycles. In some localities the specially shaped windshield which envelops the upper and bottom parts of the rider is illegal; in view of our constantly changing laws, check this out. The normal streamlined windshields are the best, of course, and well worth their cost on a high-speed motorcycle. The ordinary windshield which can be bolted to the handlebar is the most common, good for warding off rain and debris kicked up by cars and trucks. Your main concern is riding on a windy day; many riders have been surprised by the power of the wind, which can make it nearly impossible to control the machine on a straight line.

Radar detectors and CB radios are also available for mounting on your motorized bike, as are many other items. You'll have to decide what you really need and what you want for showing off—it's a matter of personal taste.

Don't Ride a Neglected Machine

2

"What," I asked my road-racing friend, "is the most important thing for a motorcycle racer before and during a race?"

He thought for only a moment, having spent many years racing successfully in Italy and the United States. He had also raced in motocross events. He said, "There are two things. You've got to be sure your bike is in absolutely top condition, so you know the machine like your own hand. And you must know how to handle *that* machine in all circumstances."

"Inspecting the machine, right?"

"Not only inspecting. Anybody can look at the bolts and the cables and say he's inspecting things. The important thing is to build up experience to spot the weak points, where things are not working the way they should. So you inspect, and you make a lot of fine adjustments. You don't fool around; after all, your life depends on that machine."

The advice of my friend holds not only for racers of motorcycles but also for riders of ordinary bicycles, mopeds, scooters, and motorcycles. Imagine what could happen in traffic if the control you needed wasn't working.

The key words are *inspect* and *adjust,* and you can do it easily on whichever machine you own. Make sure the important parts of your two-wheeler are working the way they should. As you use your machine, cables will stretch and nuts and bolts will loosen. You must notice this in time and take care of it—*your first step toward safe riding.*

Light bulbs can blow out and fuel and oil can disappear, unnoticed. It's up to you to keep track of things because they are not going to take care of themselves.

Before starting out for any ride, quickly check the following:
Tires, Wheels, Axles
Hand Brake Levers (Foot Brake on scooters and motorcycles)
Handlebar
Chain
Seat
Horn or Bell
All Lights, Mirrors, Reflectors
Bicycle Gear Shifters
Fuel and Oil (on motorized two-wheelers)

And you'll need some simple tools with which to make adjustments.

BASIC TOOLS

A small and a large adjustable wrench, even if your machine comes with a set of tools. A small and a large screwdriver. A pair of pliers. A hand pump and a tire pressure gauge. A tube valve tool and a tube patching kit, including tire-removing irons. If you're planning a long trip, be sure to have a chain repair tool and some spare links. For motorized machines, you'll need a spark plug wrench and gap feelers. Tools are not expensive, and your dealer can help select the right ones for your machine. Some machines come with a set of tools designed for that particular bike, so that one tool often does the job of several. Always carry tools with you because your fingers are limited without them.

TIRES, WHEELS, AXLES

Tire pressure is important. Racers carefully check pressure before a race because they know it must be just right. Riding on very soft tires gives you a mushy ride with poor control in curves. When you have to lean hard unexpectedly, you'll run the risk of losing control. And if your wheel hits a deep rut or a rock, a soft tire will not protect the wheel rim from damage.

A defective tube valve or a nail or cut in the tire can cause air leakage. You can replace a defective valve yourself. Unscrew the valve from inside the stem (using a valve tool—the top end of some valve caps serves this purpose); screw in the new valve tightly; then simply pump up the tire to the pressure recommended by your owner's handbook. Because a new valve could leak air, check it by placing a little saliva over the open end and watching for air bubbles. If the valve is good, be sure to replace the cap.

Gas station pumps are all right for mopeds, scooters, and motorcycles. But for a bicycle, it's best to use a hand pump instead, to avoid causing a blowout.

Riding on very hard tires gives a bouncy ride that can easily throw you out of control. Look up the recommended tire pressure for your machine, and then check them at least once every week. You'll feel the difference when you're riding and suddenly have to take evasive action. A hard tire will bounce and slide; a soft tire will send you swaying back and forth.

On bicycles, tire pressures will be anywhere from about 30 psi (pounds per square inch) to 90 psi. The average moped and scooter may require about 24 psi for the front tire and perhaps 28 or 33 psi for the rear. Depending on the weight and type of tire, a motorcycle will use from about 28 in the front and up to 36 in the rear.

Don't guess. Look up the correct tire pressure in your owner's handbook. Fortunately, many tire manufacturers emboss the sidewalls with the pressure requirements.

When your tire goes flat, so will your enthusiasm for riding, but a fix is easy enough and will put you right back on the road. To fix a flat, you'll need the patching kit: scraper, patches, glue, tire irons (don't use screwdrivers to pry a tire off the rim), bead lubricant, and an air pump. You may also need to remove the wheel, and the exact method will be described by the manufacturer in your owner's handbook.

Generally, you will not have any problems removing either the front or the rear wheel because in most instances the manufacturers have designed easy drop-out systems. Remove one axle bolt and washer, pull the axle (spindle) out the other way, and the wheel drops out. The most you may have to do is disconnect the brake cable at the wheel brake lever. This system is used on mopeds, scooters, and motorcycles. On a bicycle this won't be necessary because in most cases the tire can be squeezed through the caliper brake pads.

To find the air leak, look for the nailhead along the outside of the tire. If you find it, pull out the nail, and mark the spot. Let out all the air (open the valve by unscrewing it, or press it in), and then, with the wheel flat on the ground, stand on the edge of the tire all around in order to loosen the tire from the wheel rim. Now, apply the bead lubricant and use the tire irons all around to pry the tire off the rim. Then pull the tube out partially, at the place where the nail (or the cut) is. Spoon handles make excellent tire irons for bicycles. Scrape down the area, apply glue to the patch (after removing its protective sheet), and then press it firmly and evenly over the scraped hole area. Let it dry, per instructions that come with the kit.

When you begin refitting the tube into the tire, avoid pinching the tube with the tire irons. Never use a screwdriver for this job. If you've had to remove the entire tube or to replace it with a new one, first fit the tube valve stem through the hole in the rim. A protective tube strip is inside all tires to keep the spoke ends (inside the rim) from damaging the tube, and this strip must be carefully centered all around. Use the tire irons very carefully, and plenty of bead lubricant, to avoid pinching the tire and having to repeat the job. After riding, always check the tires for possible damage by nails, glass pieces, or other debris lodged in the grooves.

While working around the wheels, check the condition of the rims and tightness of the spokes. A badly bent rim can be dangerous; loose spokes will put the wheel out of alignment, producing a wobble as you ride. After finding a loose spoke on your wheel, use a small wrench or spoke nipple tool to tighten it. Looking down at the bottom portion of the wheel nearest the ground, tighten the nipple counterclockwise.

Even on a brand-new machine, check the axle nuts for tightness, especially on bicycles. If your bicycle is equipped with quick-release hubs, make sure the levers are closed tightly and facing to the rear. If they face forward, they could conceivably hook into something and open, causing the wheel to fall off.

The front and rear forks (rear swing arm) on mopeds and scooters are suspended on springed shock absorbers. Bounce the machine, and listen for noises to see if a spring is broken. Hydraulic suspension systems are used on motorcycles, and if the fluid leaks out of the cylinders, your control will be affected. Check periodically; listen for clanking sounds, and look for leakage. Also check your Parts List booklet to understand better the suspension system on your particular machine.

HAND AND FOOT BRAKE LEVERS

Whether you squeeze hand brake levers or step on the foot brake lever, you're forcing brake pads against the wheel rim or disc or brake shoes inside the hub against the drum.

To check the action of the brake, put your weight on the handlebar, and push the machine forward, squeezing the brake lever or pressing hard against the foot brake lever. If the wheel does not stop instantly, the brake is working improperly and will be worth little when needed for a panic stop. Test the other brake the same way. Just how far must you squeeze the hand brake lever to get the brake to hold solidly? If the lever, when squeezed, touches the handlebar itself, you're in danger. A clearance of at least one inch should be between the lever and the handlebar when you squeeze hard.

This "soft brake" condition is common on any brake system which uses cables between the lever and the brake arm. As they're used, cables stretch a bit, and you'll need to take up the slack. Simply follow the cable to find a holding nut, or knurled ring, where the cable either emerges from the hand brake lever or is attached to the arm of the brake system at the wheel hub. This is your adjustment point.

On bicycles, caliper brakes are of the side-pull or center-pull type, and the holding nut is where the cable comes down from the hand lever. Loosen the holding nut as you squeeze the brake pad arms

After loosening the cable-holding nut on the side-pull caliper-type brake, squeeze the pads against the wheel rim, pull the slack cable until taut, and tighten the cable-holding nut, visible at the tip of the pliers.

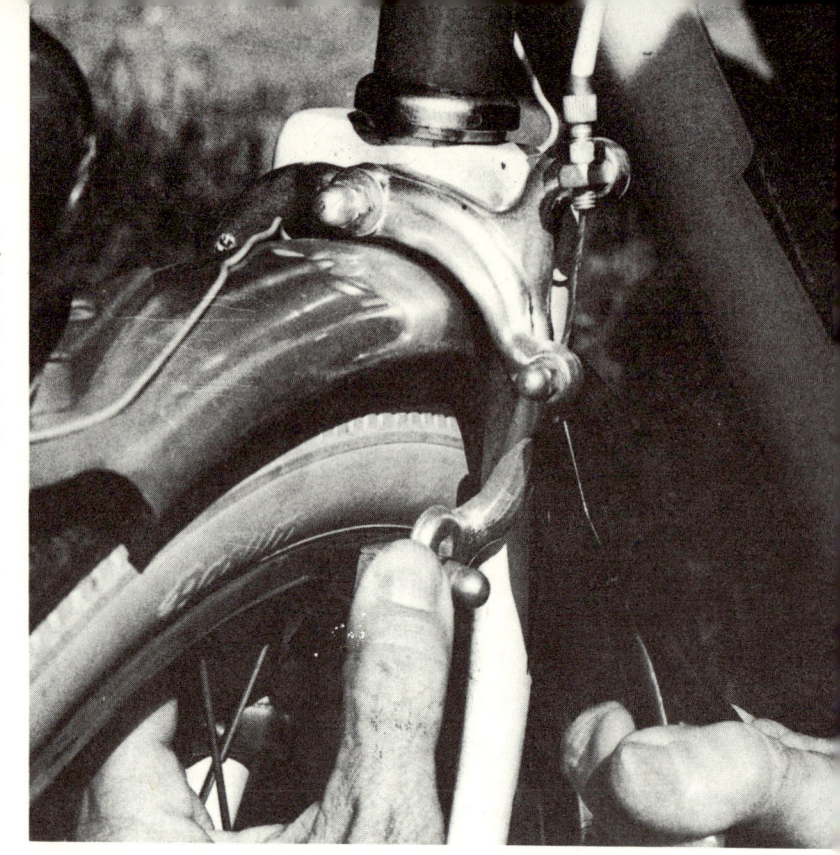

Loosen the locknut and turn the adjusting barrel for fine adjustments. Then be sure to retighten the locknut. Never oil the wheel rims.

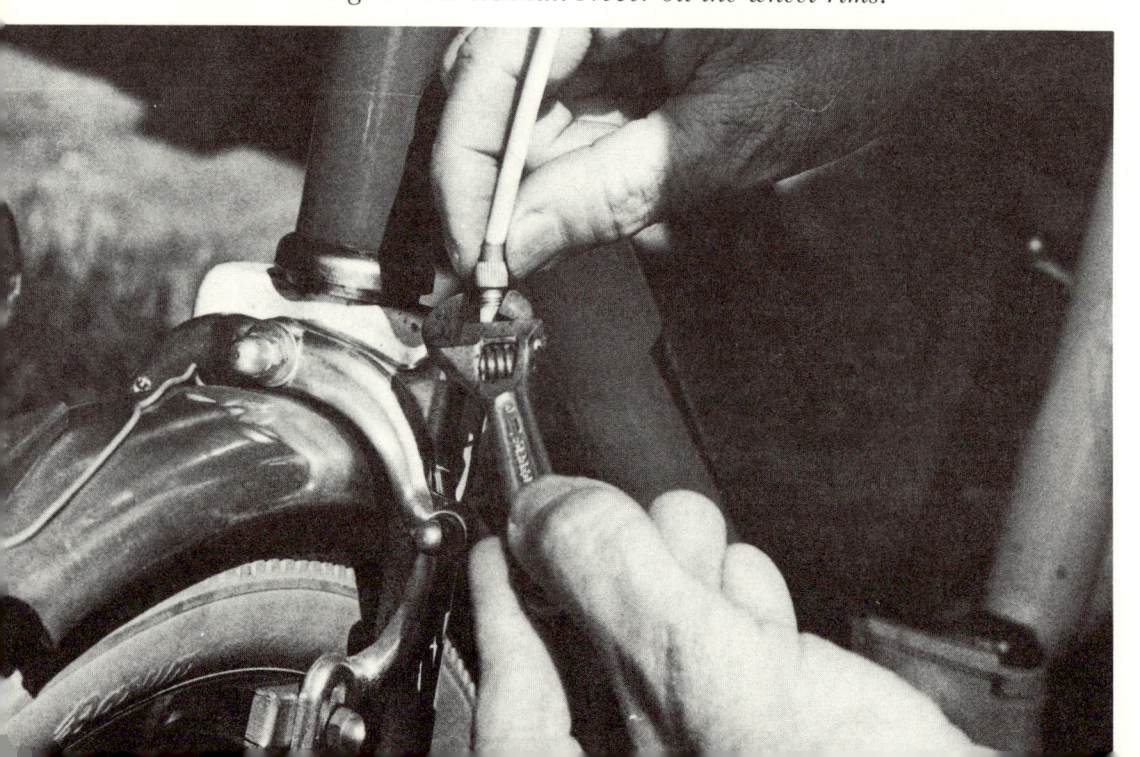

If the brake pads are off-center, loosen the backside mounting nut (not the front acorn-type nut) and move the brake mechanism so neither pad rubs the rim. Then retighten the backside nut firmly.

The center-pull calipers also have a brake cable-holding nut for taking up cable slack. Note the cable connection between the two brake arms.

The cable slack at the bridge can also be adjusted. You'll need a friend or inexpensive brake-squeezer tool when loosening and tightening the cable-holding nuts.

against the rim of the wheel, using either your fingers or the inexpensive "squeezer" tool designed for the job. Then let a friend pull the cable tight, or do it yourself, using the "squeezer" tool. Now just tighten the holding nut, and let go of the brake arms. Spin the wheel to make sure the brake pads are scraping neither the rim nor the tire itself.

If the brake pads are not centered, either pad can rub against the rim. To center the entire mechanism, loosen the backside mounting nut at the spot where the mechanism is fastened to the wheel fork.

Make sure the coaster brake arm is fastened securely to the frame chain stay by the bolt and clamp.

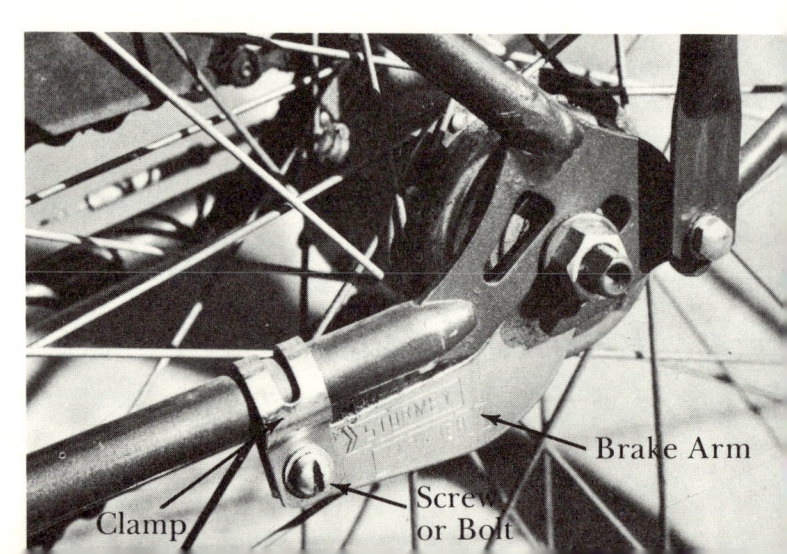

Brake Arm
Screw or Bolt
Clamp

Carefully move the entire mechanism slightly to center it, and again tighten the backside nut securely. Then test it.

Single-speed bicycles, and sometimes 3-speed models, are fitted with a coaster brake at the rear wheel. On these types make sure the small curved brake arm at the rear hub is fastened to the fork arm (chain stay). No adjustment can be made on a coaster brake, so if pressure against the pedals is not bringing you to a stop, have a bicycle repair shop change the hub.

On Shimano bicycle rear wheel disc brakes, pad clearance adjustments are made with the adjusting barrel to which the cable is fastened. Never oil or apply polish to a disc.

On most motorized bikes, brake cable slack can be taken up at the brake arm by turning a convenient large wing nut or bolt. On this Jawa motorcycle, note the brake-shoe wear-gauge pointer.

For the front brake, fine adjustments can be made at the handlebar brake lever by loosening the lockring and turning the barrel. A similar setup can be found on mopeds. Always leave a bit of free play for the lever. (Clutch-cable slack adjuster is at the clutch lever on the left handlebar.)

The Pacer moped provides cable slack and fine adjustment right at the front brake hub. Note the inspection holes for checking brake shoe wear.

The rear wheel brake cable can be easily tightened and secured by the cable-holding nut. The same setup is used on most scooters and motorcycles, as are the chain-tension adjusters.

These front and rear perforated disc brakes on the 1000cc BMW ensure reliable stops at any speed. The sophisticated suspension system ensures control on any surface.

    If your bicycle is equipped with a disc brake, you'll find a knurled nut (with a locknut) for adjustment purposes. Make sure that the pads grip the disc when you apply the brake and that the pads are not rubbing against the disc when you're riding.

    On mopeds, scooters, and motorcycles the brake arm is at the wheel hub, front and rear, and forces the brake shoes to expand against the wheel drum inside the hub. Adjustment is by means of a large wing nut and is easy to do. Make sure that the brake is not dragging, that its action is powerful, and that the wheel is not wobbling. Fine adjustments can be made at the hand brake lever. On scooters and motorcycles the rear wheel brake is worked by the right foot. The usual connection is by a rod, with the adjustment nut at the end of the rod where it connects to the brake arm.

Many motorcycles are fitted with powerful "self-adjusting" disc brakes at the front and sometimes at the rear. The exact method of adjusting, as well as the care and maintenance of the hydraulic fluid system used, can be found in the owner's handbook.

Remember the warning about brakes: on bicycles, do *not* use any kind of oil or polish on the wheel rims (if you have caliper brakes) or the disc (if you have disc brakes). Do *not* let oil or grease get onto the brake shoes or drum of a moped, scooter, or motorcycle brake or onto the discs, if so equipped. If you run through deep water or have been riding in rain, your brakes will work less effectively than when they're totally dry.

HANDLEBARS

Make sure your handlebar cannot be pushed up and down freely or twisted sideways (while the front wheel faces forward). On a bicycle, keep the stem bolt tightened. This bolt is at the top center of the

To raise or lower the handlebar on your bicycle, first loosen the stem bolt (here the hammer is resting on it) and strike it downward to loosen the inside wedge. Be sure to tighten the stem bolt after adjusting the handlebar.

44 / *Fun and Safety on Two Wheels*

handlebar and goes into the front wheel fork tube. If for any reason you want to remove the handlebar from the fork, loosen this stem bolt, place a pad on top of it to protect the chrome finish, and with a hammer strike downward against the bolt to loosen the wedge inside the fork tube.

The same stem bolt is found on some mopeds but not on scooters or motorcycles. Depending on the model machine, the handlebar can be raised or lowered to suit your comfort and can also be tilted up or down to give the best position for riding. The adjustment is simple, through the use of bolts and clamps, but be sure to tighten these bolts after resetting the angle and position of the handlebar.

Do not ride a machine with a loose handlebar!

On the two-chain model moped (like this Jawa), the tension of the main chain and the pedaling chain can be adjusted with the respective adjusters. Be sure to retighten the nuts.

Easy chain tensioning on motorcycles is by means of adjusters at the rear axle, as shown on this Jawa. In all cases turn the adjusters equally on both sides so the wheel remains straight.

CHAINS

A link can snap on an old worn chain, preventing you from pedaling or, in the case of motorized two-wheelers, from controlling engine power to the rear wheel. On the other hand, a loose chain can ride right off the sprockets (gears). And a tight chain can damage itself, the sprockets, and the bearings.

To check the tension of a chain, use a stick and press down at the midpoint of the top part. If it gives more than a half inch, it's a loose chain, and if less than a quarter of an inch, it's too tight. Don't use this test on 5- and 10-speed bicycles because the bottom tension pulley of the rear derailleur keeps the chain properly tensioned.

To adjust the chain for correct tension, first loosen the axle bolts of the rear wheel, and then move the rear wheel either forward or backward, as the case may be. On a bicycle, simply force the rear wheel backward by wedging a piece of solid wood between the tire and the fork (to tighten the chain), or gently tap the wheel forward (to loosen the chain). After setting the tension, be sure to tighten the axle bolts evenly on both sides, and then check the wheel for possible wobble.

On motorized machines, adjusters hold the rear axle in correct position, so after loosening the main axle bolts, loosen the locknuts on the adjusters and turn each adjuster the same amount to tension the chain. Spin the wheel to make sure that the axle is evenly spaced and that there is no wobble; securely tighten the axle bolts and the locknuts on the adjusters. Before starting work on these adjusters, study them carefully or read about them in your owner's handbook.

All chains (except those used on derailleurs) are closed by a master link which has a special removable clip. This allows easy opening of the chain in case of repair or replacement. To open the chain, pry off the clip and push out the master link. The chain can now be taken off the sprockets. When hooking up the new chain, replace the clip on the master link with the closed end of the clip facing forward, in the direction of chain travel.

On derailleurs the chains are of the continuous type, without a master link or clip. This is because the continuous type of chain travels smoothly through the tension and guide pulleys of the derailleur while a chain with a master link and clip would snag. Therefore, if this type of chain must be opened, one link must be forced out and its replacement must then be properly riveted in again (with a special tool). Some motorcycles also use this type of chain.

Keep a chain properly lubricated, dipping a small brush into lightweight oil and running it along the chain. Use a rag to wipe off the oil, making sure not to get any oil on the wheel rims or discs.

SEAT

I was once riding with a friend who had to stop every so often to pull the seat of his bicycle up out of the seat tube. "One of these days," he said, "I'll have to fix this." We then fixed it by setting the seat to the correct height and tightening the bolt under the seat.

The seat on your machine should be firmly in place, set for your comfort. A bicycle's seat is set in relation to the pedals, but on motorized machines your feet must be able to reach the ground when you're sitting on the seat. Having to tiptoe the ground for control because the machine is too high for you is extremely dangerous, so never ride any machine that's not fitted to your foot reach. Recently I was in a motorcycle shop where the salesperson was holding the machine steady because the buyer could barely touch the floor with his toes (maybe they planned to fit smaller wheels to the bike later on!).

HORN OR BELL

Check the horn's working condition before every ride. Don't use it continually; instead, sound off only for an emergency. Use it to announce your presence when another driver seems unaware of you. The horn is a signaling device to be used for special occasions, rather than a noisemaker.

LIGHTS, REFLECTORS, MIRRORS

Keep all reflectors and mirrors clean, as well as the glass of the front and rear light.

On motorized machines, start up the engine, and then switch on the lights. Test the high-beam switch and the electrical direction signals (these can be found on scooters and motorcycles, and sometimes mopeds, as optional items).

Check that the stoplight at the rear is working when you use the hand brake levers or the foot brake. It's easy enough to replace a bad bulb or a blown fuse or to reconnect a loose wire. Also check the condition of your scooter or motorcycle battery.

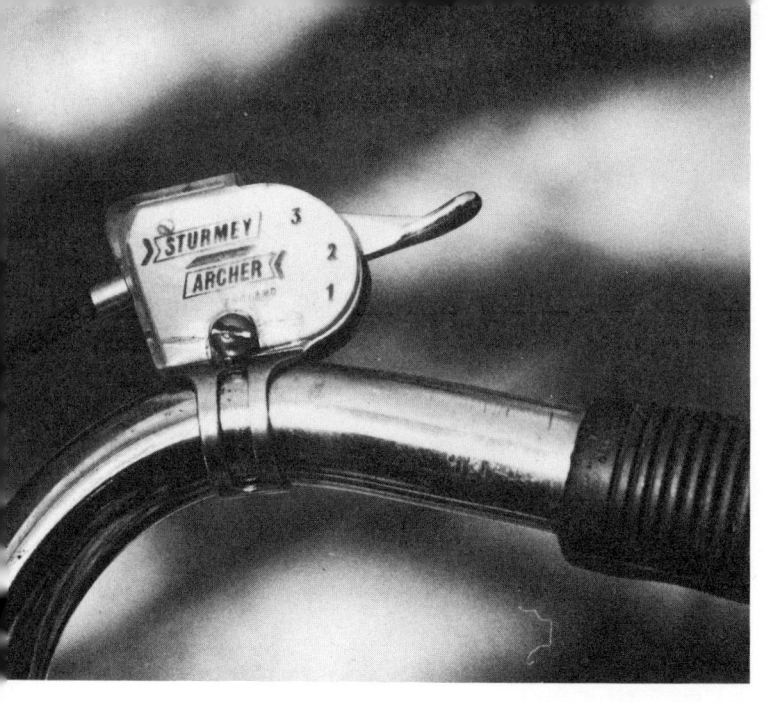

This 3-speed bicycle shifter trigger is shown in position 2 for general riding and checking adjustment. Position 1 is for starting off, riding uphill, and against wind; 3 is for high speeds.

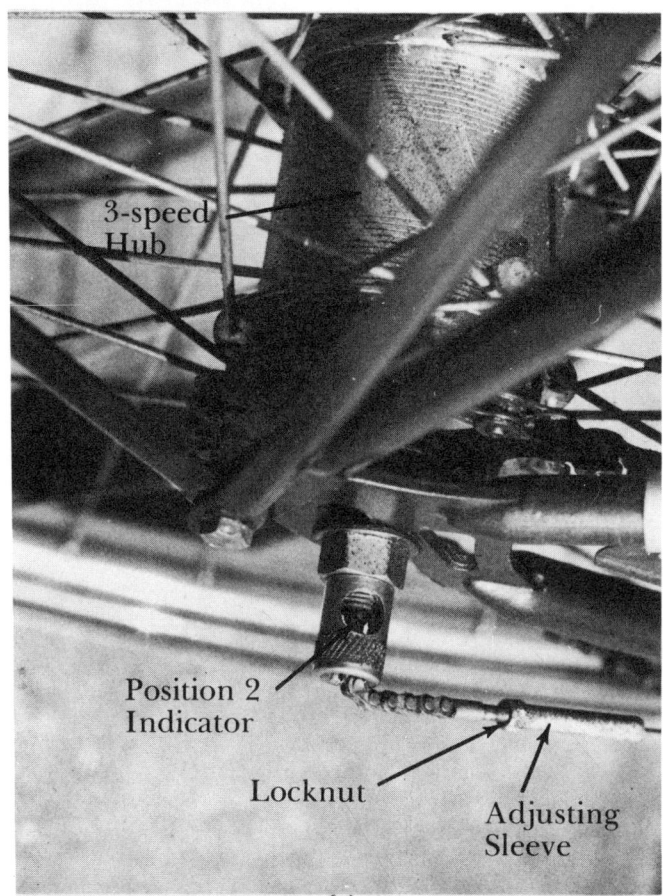

With the trigger in position 2, the indicator at the axle must be centered in the slot. Loosen the locknut and use the adjusting sleeve to center the indicator.

Don't go riding if any of these have been damaged, removed by a thief, or are working improperly.

BICYCLE GEAR SHIFTERS

Some riders using a 3-speed bicycle huff and puff uphill in gear number 3, not realizing that gear number 1 is used for hills.

In another instance a bicyclist can't understand why the chain is falling off the rear sprocket every time he tries to shift to another gear.

What are the possible problems in shifting a 3-speed bicycle? The shifting control may be either a trigger or a twistgrip, on the right handlebar. Both types are marked *1 or L* to mean first or low gear (used to go up a hill or into a strong wind), *2 or N* to indicate middle or normal gear (used for general riding on level ground), and *3 or H* for top or high gear (used for pedaling at high speed).

When you move the trigger or twistgrip to one of these positions, a cable pulls a short chain or an L-shaped bar (bell crank) at the rear wheel hub. Ride the bike, and set the trigger or twistgrip at the 2 or N position; then stop to check the indicator bar at the wheel hub. If prolonged use has stretched the cable or if the holding nut has let the cable slip a bit, the index mark of the indicator bar (a simple notch, the letter *N* or *O*) will not line up in the slot. If this is the case, loosen the locking nut just ahead of the knurled sleeve attached to the cable, and watch the index mark move in the slot. Center the index mark, and tighten the locking nut at the adjusting sleeve. Ride the bike around, and use the shifter; set it again at 2 or N, and check it. A small readjustment may be necessary. Remember to move the trigger or the twistgrip as you're pedaling along easily, not when you're straining against the pedals.

In the case of a 5-speed or 10-speed model, the chain must be moving through the derailleur as you shift. Unfortunately the chain may tend to slip off the smallest sprocket (toward the outside of the bike) or off the largest sprocket (toward the inside) at the rear wheel and on a 10-speeder may tend to fall off one of the front sprockets (chain wheels).

The remedy is simple. Set your bike upside down so it rests on the

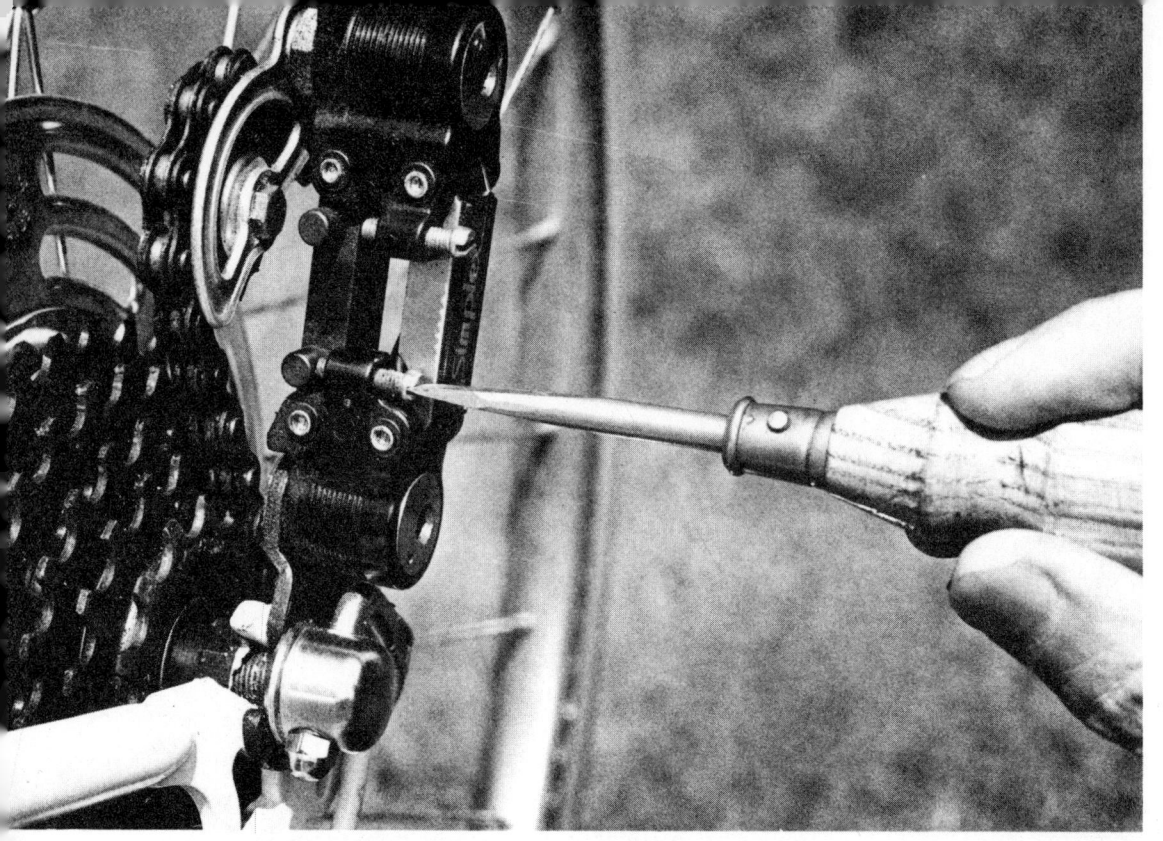

To adjust derailleurs easily, set the bike upside down. Crank the pedals to keep the chain moving, using the shifter to get the chain on the smallest sprocket (gear), as shown. The stop screw must now be firmly against the stop block. Note gap of top stop screw to its stop block: make the same adjustment.

seat and the handlebar, and start cranking the pedals by hand so the chain turns the rear wheel. The chain must be moving before you try shifting. Very slowly, move the right-side shift lever *forward,* and watch the chain ride down onto the smallest sprocket, which is the highest gear. (Rarely is the lever moved backward for high gear, but some bikes do have this arrangement.) When the chain is riding on the smallest gear, use the brake to stop the wheel. Now check the position of the two stop screws against the stop blocks at the rear derailleur mechanism. One screw, the high gear adjuster, will nearly or actually touch the block, while the other screw and block, the low gear adjuster, will be far from touching.

The stop screws and stop blocks simply control the limit of movement (how far inward and how far outward the derailleur will move). This is their only function; that is why they are so easy to adjust. On different model bicycles these screws and blocks can be found in different positions. On one imported model, only one screw is used for both high and low gear adjustment.

Check the position of these screws against the blocks when the chain is on the gear in question, and make sure the stop screw will not allow the derailleur to move any farther in or out, thus preventing the chain from falling off the respective sprocket. Similarly, if the chain cannot be made to go onto the smallest or the largest sprocket, the stop screw is already up against the stop block and does not allow the mechanism to move far enough to make the gear change possible. Simply loosen the respective stop screw.

After setting up the shifter, start cranking the pedal by hand and

Whenever tension at the shift lever is too loose, the chain will keep dropping onto high gear. The remedy is to tighten the friction nut, as shown here.

move the shift lever forward as far as it will go. It the chain goes onto the smallest sprocket and does not fall off, you've got a good adjustment. Continue cranking and move the shift lever all the way backward. The chain should ride up onto the largest sprocket without falling off. If the chain misbehaves, you now know how to make adjustments at the stop blocks. If the shifting is without a problem, as outlined, but the cable is slightly loose after the chain is on the smallest sprocket, simply take up the slack by loosening the cable-holding nut right at the derailleur mechanism, and pull the cable taut.

Another sneaky situation is when the chain keeps dropping to the smallest sprocket, with no help from you. While riding along, you shift to one of the middle gears, and suddenly the chain slips to high gear without your ever touching the shift lever. This is because the friction nut in the center of the shifting lever is loose. This friction nut may be a screw or a wing nut. It keeps the lever in its set place, through friction. Tighten it so it will hold, but not so tight that the lever can't be moved.

The adjustment for the front derailleur is the same—a screw or nut which prevents the chain cage from being moved too far in or out. Even the best adjustment may loosen in time and need to be checked. Shifting a derailleur calls for some practice—there are no notches or marked positions, and therefore, shifting is really done by feel. Move the lever slightly as you pedal along, and listen to the chain climbing up or dropping down, one sprocket at a time.

Mopeds, scooters, and motorcycles run on gasoline, and the engine must be lubricated with oil; therefore, before starting out, check the fuel and oil.

FUEL AND OIL

Don't take the gas tank, gearbox, and crankcase for granted. They do not replenish themselves, so you should remove the gas tank cap to check the gas level visually and should pull out the dipstick (or open the oil level screw) to check the oil. Have you any idea how many people have tried to start an engine with a dry tank? Or how many perfectly good engines have been ruined because somebody ran them without oil?

If you run out of gas on a moped, you could pedal it to the nearest gas station, but this soon becomes tiring. If you should have to pedal a moped, remember that (on some models) you can disconnect the engine and use the pedals as you would on a bicycle.

"Just a moment," you say triumphantly. "These machines have a reserve position on their fuel valves. All I have to do is switch over, and I'm on my way."

Quite true, but many a rider has switched to reserve, filled the gas tank, and continued along, forgetting to set the fuel valve back to its regular open position. As the gas in the tank, including the reserve supply, was used up completely, there was no reserve fuel left. Have you ever had to push a heavy motorcycle?

Check the gas each time you start out, and if you use the reserve fuel and then fill up, be sure to set the fuel valve back to the regular open position.

Check the oil, too. On a four-stroke engine, check the crankcase oil level, and on both the four-stroke and two-stroke engines check the gearbox oil. The fuel for two-stroke engines is a mixture of gas and oil, well mixed in the correct proportion as recommended by the manufacturer.

These primary checks will put you ahead of those who trust to luck and memory. You should make up your own list of checks and precautions and use them to feel safe while riding. You'll be in a class with the professionals.

Know Your Engine

3

An engine that is not operating properly can easily contribute to an accident. Before you handle the throttle, pull the clutch, or shift the gears, you should have a good understanding of how the engine and drive system work.

On a bicycle you take care of the gear changing mechanism because it's the part that keeps you going; on a motorized machine you take care of the engine because an efficiently running engine promotes a feeling of security, which means safe riding.

The job of any engine is a simple one: to keep the crankshaft turning. Through this, the chain keeps the rear wheel turning. If the engine stops, so does everything else.

A friend of mine was barreling along on his 900 cc motorcycle, enjoying the sound of the purring engine beneath him, keeping his eyes on the cars around and ahead of him, both hands on the grips, knees relaxed, and feet on the pegs. Suddenly the engine died. He pulled the clutch to keep rolling, and wondered which car would plow into him. In such situations car drivers don't expect a car or motorcycle to slow down suddenly because they're really not prepared for the unexpected. My friend found it safer to cut to the left, off the concrete and onto the grass divider. After he calmed down, he began checking things—tank half full, fuel valve open, plug wires connected, all other wiring connected. What he finally discovered (after making sure he had a spark and that the fuel line was feeding) was a speck of dirt closing off the carburetor jet. He cleaned this and

56 / *Fun and Safety on Two Wheels*

went on his way. In this case the engine failure was caused by something which every rider tries to minimize through periodic maintenance of fuel lines, filters, and the carb. It was probably his riding experience that gave him the presence of mind to pull the clutch and luckily get off the road.

Since dirt of any kind is notorious for stopping engines, make it a habit to check the fuel and air filters every so often. This is especially true on two-stroke engines because the gas-oil mixture frequently cakes up on the fine wire mesh fuel filter. Simply drain the tank, take out the filter (usually a part of the fuel valve), let it dry thoroughly,

Clean the moped air filter periodically for efficient engine operation. This is the Pacer, but other mopeds have other types of filters, sometimes located elsewhere.

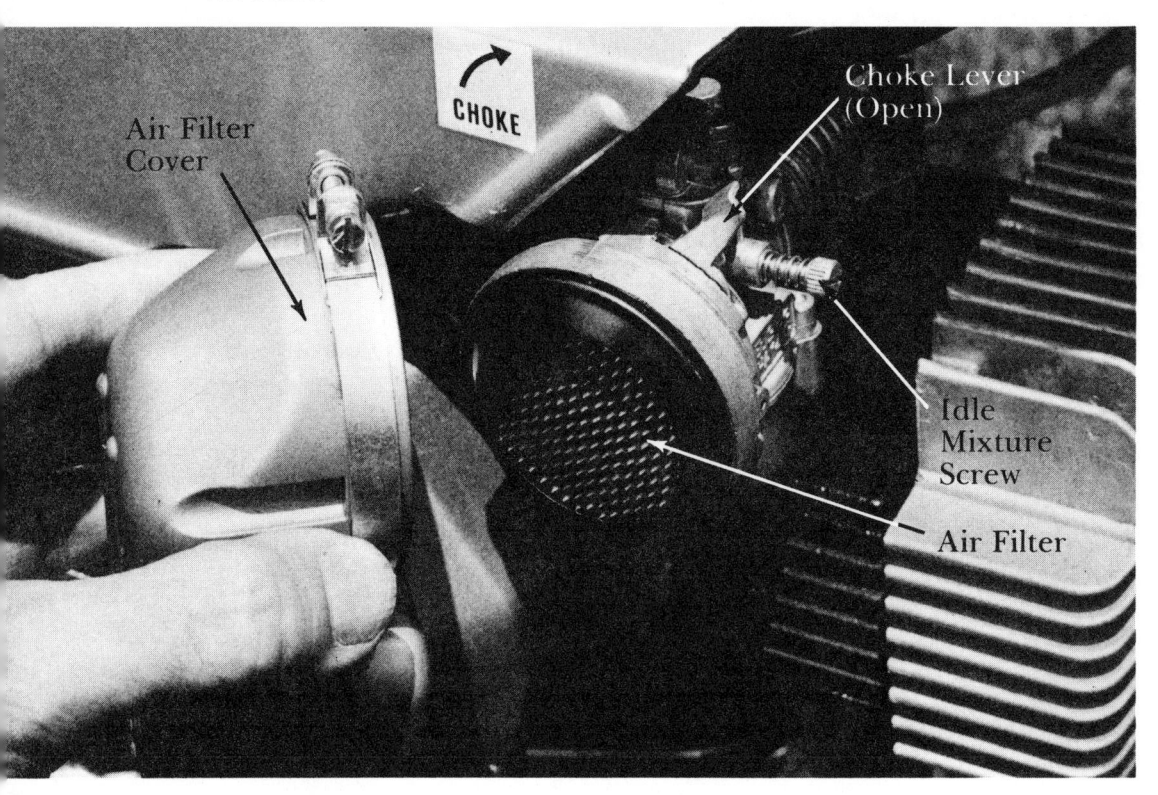

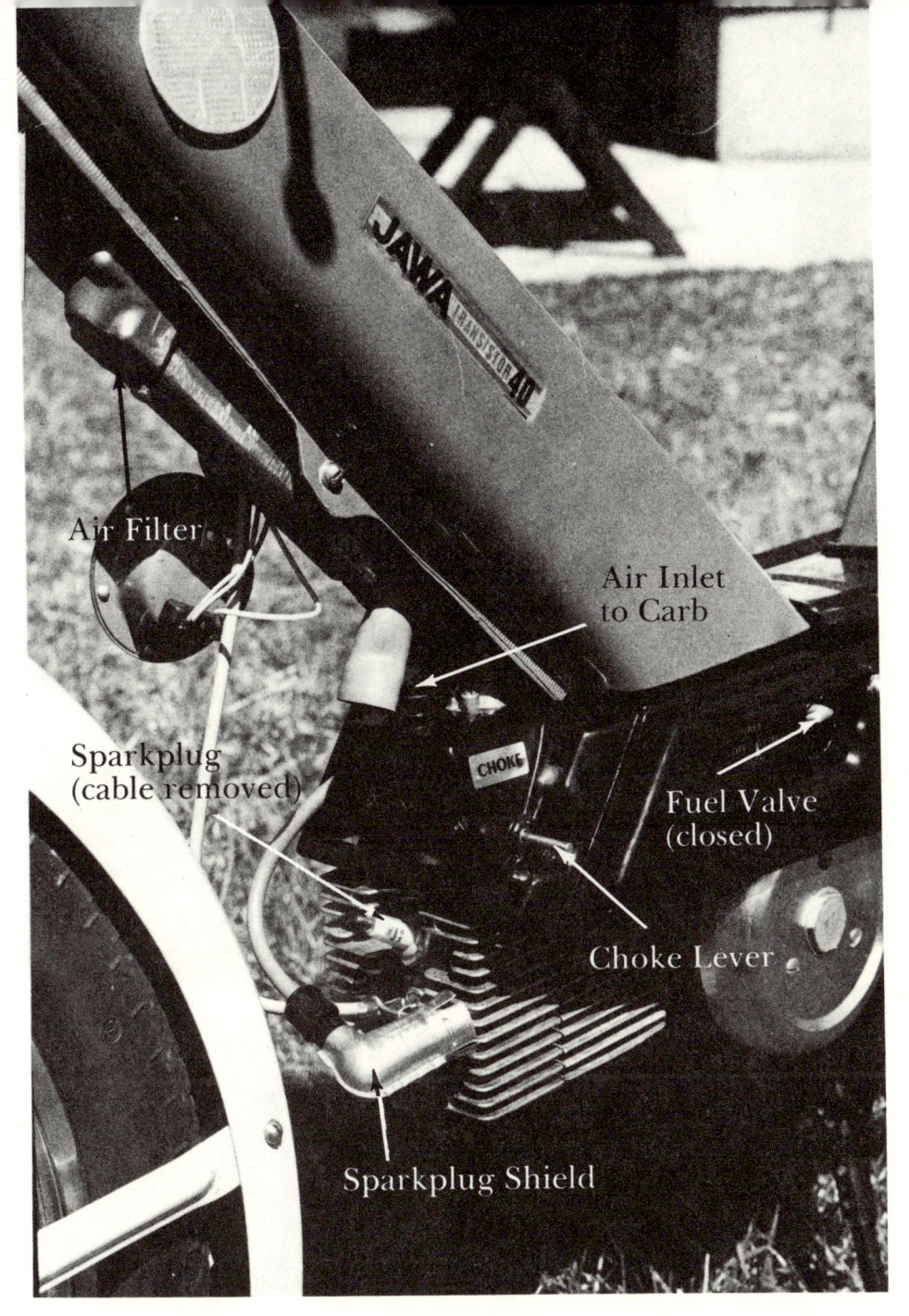

The Jawa moped air filter is under the tank, with the connecting hose loosened to show the air inlet to the carb. The fuel filter is part of the fuel valve on this model.

Here, the Pacer air filter has been removed, with the choke closed to cut off air to the carb (rich mixture). The idle adjusting screw is visible next to the choke lever. Note the cylinder cooling fins.

and tap it against a hard surface to dislodge the dirt. Clean out the gas tank once a year, using your owner's handbook for the correct procedure. Some fuel valves contain a removable filter, in which case the tank need not be drained.

Before the 55 mph speed law was imposed, another friend was doing over 80 on an open stretch, while I rode behind him. Suddenly he veered, straightened out, then pulled off the road. It turned out his engine had seized completely. What had saved him from a spill

The Jawa choke is open and a screwdriver is in the fuel/air mixture control screw. The screw above it is the idle adjuster.

was the good habit of riding with both hands on the handlebar and the fingers of his left hand resting over the clutch lever. When the engine froze, he had the presence of mind to squeeze and coast off. This kind of problem cannot be fixed by cleaning dirt out of the carb as in the previous incident. Instead, it required a complete—and expensive—disassembling of the engine to free and repair the damaged parts.

Any engine will seize if it is run without enough lubrication for the moving parts. On a four-stroker, check the crankcase and gearbox oil levels by pulling out the dipstick occasionally. If it needs oil, add it, making sure it's the kind recommended by the manufacturer. On a two-stroker, be sure to mix properly the right kind of oil with the gas in the tank and to check the gearbox oil level. The crankcase of a two-stroker is lubricated automatically. On some model scooters and motorcycles a system of automatic oil injection is used, eliminating the need to mix gas and oil manually.

Periodically check the amount of oil in the gearbox. Use a dipstick or level check hole.

A simplified automatic oil injector delivers the correct amount of two-stroke oil to the gas to create the proper fuel mixture in the carb of this Jawa 350cc, eliminating the need to mix the fuel manually.

Mopeds use two-stroke engines. The usual fuel mixture is one part oil to 20 or 30 parts gas, mixed well before pouring into the tank.

Oil is the lifeblood of the engine, lubricating the critical parts in order to keep them working. It also serves as a cooler, reducing the heat caused by friction. Lubrication keeps the heat under control and the engine at efficient operating temperatures.

Old, worn-out oil does little good for the engine. Therefore, at recommended intervals warm up the engine, shut it off, drain the old oil out, and refill the crankcase and/or gearbox. Thereafter make it a habit to check the cases for possible leakage.

On some new motorcycles with liquid-cooled engines check frequently for coolant leakage because if a leak should develop, the engine will overheat, as it would on a car.

Virtually all mopeds use a two-stroke engine that has a 50 cc displacement (engine size in metric measure) and produces from 1 to 2 horsepower (hp). The fuel for all two-strokers is a mixture of regular gas and special oil; this means that about five ounces of two-stroke oil are added to one gallon of gas, mixed well, and poured into the moped tank. The gas-oil proportion is usually stamped on the gas tank for easy reference or given in your owner's handbook.

Since oil settles, it's a good idea to shake the moped from side to side *before* you start the engine so the oil and gas will be well mixed again. This mixture of gas and oil also serves to lubricate the engine: therefore, on mopeds you don't have to check the oil supply in the crankcase (the crankshaft is lubricated automatically). But do check the oil in the gearbox.

Two-stroke engines are also used on scooters and motorcycles, especially machines used for certain kinds of racing. These engines are a marvel of simplicity, even when they employ automatic oil injection systems. They have no camshafts, pushrods, rockers, valves, or oil pumps, with nothing more than a piston connected to the crankshaft and a cylinder with intake, exhaust, and transfer portholes. The spark plug fires on every second stroke, the engine thus producing tremendous *torque* or power.

All four-stroke engines (used on some scooters, and most motorcycles) fire once in every four strokes and therefore need the cams, rods, rockers, and valves for the intake, compression, power,

This is the dynamo and transistorized (no breaker points) ignition on a Class C Jawa moped.

Shown here are the breaker points and condensers of the usual battery and coil ignition system. Many motorcycles are equipped with alternators or generators. Note the clutch cable, lever, and adjuster, left of the dynamo.

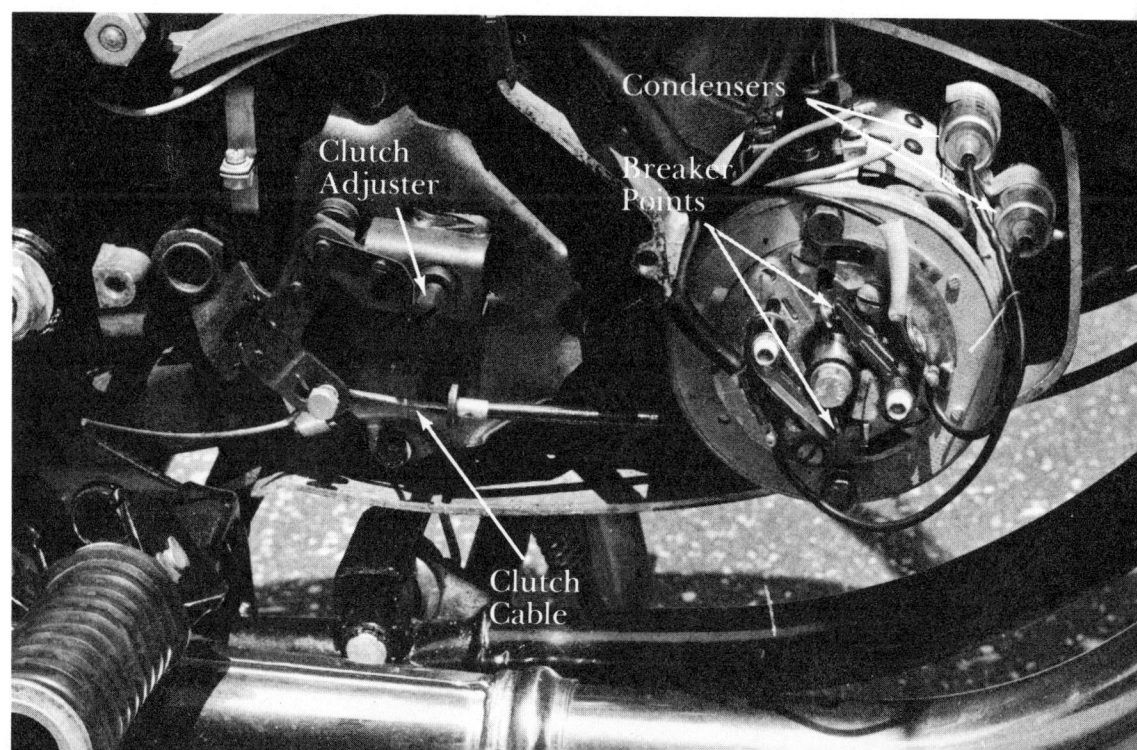

and exhaust strokes. These engines feed on regular or high-test gas, with no oil added. But check the crankcase and gearbox oil levels from time to time, as well as the manufacturer's recommendations on the kind of gas to be used.

All engines use a carburetor (carb) which mixes fuel with air: about 15 parts of air to 1 part of fuel, in the form of a vapor. This mixture is then ignited by the spark plug of the ignition system, in some cases battery and coil (with contact breakers and condenser), or a self-contained magneto, or flywheel dynamo, or a transistorized ignition (which does not use a mechanical contact breaker).

Timing of the spark for combustion must take place at precisely the right instant as the piston compresses the fuel mixture in the cylinder. Therefore, all starting and running problems, except for mechanical failure, are caused by either carburetion or ignition.

ENGINE ABUSE
This unnecessary practice has become a habit among riders who either don't know what they're doing or just don't care how much money they spend on repairs.

"But," you ask, "how is it possible to abuse an engine when it's made of tough steel and machined to close tolerances to make sure every part fits perfectly? All it does is turn the crankshaft. What could you do to hurt it?"

The tough steel parts, machined to close tolerances, are what can be hurt. "But aren't the parts being protected by the lubricating oil?" you may ask. Oil does protect the moving parts, but it's still possible to abuse the engine by not handling it the right way, especially when it's new.

It's important to baby the engine until it's broken in. Be sure it's warmed up before starting out, take it easy for the first 300 to 500 miles, change the oil and filters, and don't race the engine while standing still.

Engines are cooled by air, and even the few motorcycles that feature "liquid cooling" must depend on moving air to cool the radiator and engine surfaces. As friction of the moving parts inside the engine creates heat, causing the parts to expand, the close tolerances become even closer. Therefore, it's vitally important to prevent too much heat from building up too fast.

Don't admire the rider who boasts, "I fire up, jump on, and blast away!" The cold engine parts expand too fast as the heat develops suddenly, the oil has no chance to lubricate and cool, and after a few hundred miles, the complaint is: "I don't know what's wrong with my engine."

Smart riders give the engine time to warm up. Then, out on the road, they don't abuse the engine by running at high speed for long distances. Instead, they alternate between normal and occasional high-speed running, seldom faster than 50 mph. Never run an engine wide open for long distances, unless it has been properly broken in during its first 500 to 1,000 miles.

One often sees two riders stop to talk, all the while keeping their engines turning over, the cooling fins, cylinders, and other internal parts getting hotter and hotter. How much smarter and more professional it would be to shut off the engines first!

Another way of abusing an engine is to lug it. Lugging is trying to ride in the wrong gear. If you're going uphill in top gear and suddenly feel the engine straining, shift down to a lower gear. The engine revolutions will then be balanced out against the revolutions of your rear wheel, in terms of the weight carried and the hill's steepness. Lugging can also occur on level ground: moving too slowly in a high gear. Try to save your engine from this unnecessary abuse. Bicycle riders know the value of using the right sprockets, moped riders learn how to assist the engine from standstill or when going uphill by pedaling, and scooter and motorcycle riders shift down to suit the situation.

It's much healthier for an engine to run at higher rpm's (revolutions per minute) in a lower gear, as when going uphill, than to strain in a high gear at low rpm's.

THE BATTERY

All motorized two-wheelers (except most mopeds) are equipped with wet-cell batteries. They are usually located on the side of the machine or under the seat. Unfortunately many riders neglect the battery, despite their dependence on it to start the engine. It's important to keep it in a charged state, the cells filled with distilled water, and the two posts and all electrical connections clean and tight.

If you disconnect the battery cables for any reason, be sure to mark which cable goes to the positive (+) and which to the negative (−) post. Check the wiring diagram in your owner's handbook to confirm on which side the battery is grounded.

Not many mopeds use wet-cell batteries because they have flywheel dynamos, or magnetos, which supply the spark for the engine, as well as electrical power for the lights and horn. Scooters and motorcycles, however, have either a six-volt (three cells) or twelve-volt (six cells) battery, so check the electrolyte level in each cell at least once a month. The electrolyte must cover the tops of the plates, so be careful not to overfill when adding distilled water (never any acid!), using just enough to keep the plates covered.

Make sure the two cables are tightly connected, and clean away any greenish dirt that may have started to build up around the connections. Apply a light coat of Vaseline over them to prevent further dirty acid buildup.

A weak battery will not have the power to crank the self-starter (if your machine has one), so keep your battery in a fully charged state. Once the engine is running, the battery will be charged by the current generating system (a dynamo, generator, or alternator). It will not overcharge the battery because a voltage regulator is part of the charging system. Most machines today have a red telltale lamp which glows during idling speed (not charging) but goes out as soon as engine rpm's are increased (charging).

Many riders avoid an emergency caused by a weak battery by buying an inexpensive "trickle charger" that hooks up house current to the charger. To charge a battery, remove it from the machine and set it up in a well-ventilated area. Most chargers have a two-way voltage switch marked 6 volts and 12 volts. Be sure to set this switch for the voltage of your battery before hooking up the charger.

Motorcycle batteries are usually fitted under the seat, as shown, or on the side of the bike. A square white cover houses the regulator (don't tamper with it!). The round air filter element is visible inside the air box behind the carb. Remove the two bolts and the whole gas tank comes off.

Clamp the red POS (+) and the black NEG (−) connectors of the charger to the correct posts of the battery, loosen each cap on each cell, and *only then* plug the charger into a wall electrical outlet. This precaution will keep you away from the battery if it should explode.

While riding, if you suddenly notice the BAT or DYN telltale lamp light up, stop and disconnect the main fuse or disconnect the battery itself. Trace the wires to discover where the problem is: disconnected wires at the dynamo or at the regulator.

TROUBLESHOOTING

When I was new on two-wheelers, I once spent almost thirty minutes kicking over my two-cylinder four-stroker before stopping in disgust. Another motorcycle rider was sitting nearby in the garage, and at last he asked "Got any gas in the tank?"

"Sure," I said, feeling almost insulted. But to make sure, I removed the cap and peered inside, shaking the bike from side to side to see the gas sloshing. "Plenty of gas."

"Got the valve open?"

I reached under the tank, and sure enough, the valve was closed. That's the way you build up troubleshooting experience—with such highly intricate technical problems as a closed fuel valve!

There are many reasons why an engine won't fire up. Usually an engine won't start because of one or two reasons: *no fuel* from the carb to the cylinder or *no spark* in the cylinder to ignite the fuel. Sometimes both conditions exist.

A rider was once so angry over his motorcycle's not starting that he sold it very cheaply, right on the spot to a wise old-timer. The smiling buyer spent thirty minutes cleaning the breaker points and filters and putting in new spark plugs, and the engine soon ran like new! If nothing is broken inside, stick to the *no fuel* and *no spark* rule.

First check for fuel. Open the fuel valve, remove the spark plug, press your finger against the spark plug hole, and turn over the engine a few times. If fuel is flowing from the tank to the carb and to the cylinder, your finger will be wet with gas. You then must check for a spark.

If you come away with a dry finger, then fuel is not reaching the cylinder, and the problem is somewhere between the tank and the carb. Check to make sure that the vent hole in the gas tank cap is clear and not creating a vacuum, that the fuel valve is open, and that fuel is visible in the transparent plastic fuel line (if you have one) leading from the tank down to the carb inlet. Also make sure that the throttle is being opened when you turn the throttle twistgrip. If these check out, unscrew the idle adjustment screw about two turns, and crank the engine over several times, turning the idle adjustment screw (finger tight only) all the way in and back out one-half or one full turn.

Cover the spark plug hole with your finger, and again turn over the engine to see if fuel is getting into the cylinder. If not, the problem is in the carb, which will need a complete take-down to locate the fault. However, if fuel is wetting your finger, the rest of the problem is in the ignition system.

No matter how much fuel reaches the cylinder, if you have no spark to ignite it, the engine will not run. Check the basics: Is the ignition switch ON? Is the wire to the spark plug connected firmly? Can you find a disconnected wire anywhere—at the coil, regulator, battery, magneto? Check the fuse. Is the battery capable of sounding the horn and producing a bright light in the front headlight? If everything checks out all right, try the following:

Check the breaker points at the flywheel dynamo, using a thin screwdriver to lift them open carefully, and see if this produces a spark. If so, examine the points themselves (while turning over the engine) to see that they open and close. If the points produce a spark, then the fault could be in the spark plug itself. If no spark is produced, the fault could be in the coil, condenser, brushes, or wiring—and thus a job for a repair shop.

Disconnect the wire to the plug, remove the plug from the cylinder, and then reconnect the wire. Turn over the engine, and see if the plug produces a spark. If it does not, try a new spark plug. Another test is simply to disconnect the wire from the plug and hold the wire about one-quarter inch from some bare metal part of the engine, as you crank. If the ignition system is in good shape, a hot spark will jump from the wire to the metal.

ADJUSTING A CARBURETOR

In principle all carbs work the same way, and you should become familiar with the one (or twins) on your machine. A carb consists of a body, some precise holes and adjustment screws, and a throttle of some kind, with a fuel bowl, float, and needle. Since there are many variations, first study the description and explanations in your owner's handbook, especially if there are more than two carbs.

Basically, there are two adjusting screws. One controls the fuel and air flow and is turned out seldom more than two full turns from its fully seated position. The other screw may be set at an angle and controls the position of the throttle for idling.

Set the fuel/air proportion for a smoothly running engine, and then set the throttle screw for correct idling speed, which may be around 600 rpm's. If your machine has a tachometer, you can check it easily; if not, set the idle so the engine does not race or die out after you shut the throttle completely.

If you set the fuel/air mixture incorrectly, the engine will not run well. When too much air enters, you'll have a lean mixture, which is detrimental to pistons and cylinders. When too little air enters, you'll have a rich mixture, which is also bad for the engine and produces black oily exhaust pipes and poor running. To get a leaner mixture for whatever setting you have achieved on the carb, turn the fuel/air adjusting screw counterclockwise; to get a richer mixture, turn the screw inward, clockwise. It's not difficult to adjust a single carb, and when you have twins to contend with, your job is to bring them in together, adjusting first one, then the other, and then making sure both throttle valves inside the carbs are lifted (opened) evenly when you handle the twistgrip. This may pose a problem unless you have some experience, so study your particular owner's handbook, or let a good carb mechanic do the job.

STARTING UP AN ENGINE

Some riders kick over the engine once or twice to bring it to life, while others kick dozens of times, producing a mere cough out the exhaust.

Many riders don't know how to kick properly. First, set the machine up on its center stand. Whether it's a moped, scooter, or motorcycle, the kick must start at the top of the stroke, so that the piston is just ahead of the point when the spark ignites the fuel vapor. Set the pedal, or kick starter lever, up high so you can feel the resistance of the compression inside the cylinder; then kick down forcefully, putting your weight into it. Kick hard and without hesitation.

In winter: Open the fuel valve, and close the choke. If your carb has a tickler, press it down gently about three to six times to flood the carb. Be sure the ignition is off. Use the pedal or kick starter to turn over the engine about three times, so that the piston sucks in fuel; hold the twistgrip half open while you turn over the engine. Set the piston on compression (starter lever up high), switch the ignition on, and kick down hard. In nearly all instances this method will start up a cold engine, be it a two-stroke or four-stroke type.

Unfortunately, using the tickler or the choke too much will flood the carb and on a two-stroker will even foul the plug, which must then be taken out and cleaned. If you flood the carb, shut off the fuel valve, turn the ignition off, open the throttle wide, and kick the engine over several times to clear out the gas. Then start all over.

In summer: Use the same method, except use the tickler only once, if at all. The closed choke should be enough to start up.

In both instances, once the engine fires up, let it run at idle speed awhile to warm up; then open the choke (which is automatic on most mopeds). Don't race the engine to warm it up. Some carbs may have a choke and no tickler; others, a tickler and no choke. Both give a richer mixture for starting and warm-up and should not be used after that. After you find the right combination for starting your engine, stick to it.

In warmer weather, or if the engine has been used a few moments before shutdown, a moped engine can be started by pedaling. On some models there is a clutch lever on the left handlebar. Open the fuel valve, set the ignition on, and start pedaling. As you gather some speed, squeeze the clutch lever in order to engage the engine, holding the throttle slightly open. As soon as the engine starts, release the clutch lever, and the automatic clutch will engage.

Other moped models may have a decompression lever, in which case the same actions are performed, except that you press this lever while pedaling; this makes it easier. When the engine fires up, release the decompression lever.

To stop a moped engine, turn the ignition switch off or press the decompression lever (which opens a small valve in the cylinder and kills piston compression). Do not squeeze the clutch lever on clutch model mopeds to stop the engine.

On this Jawa motorcycle the foot shift lever also serves as the kick starter. Press the lever toward the engine, then lift up and around to the rear.

When you kick-start, kick down hard from the top, as if you wanted to reach the ground. Be sure the fuel valve is open and the ignition is switched on.

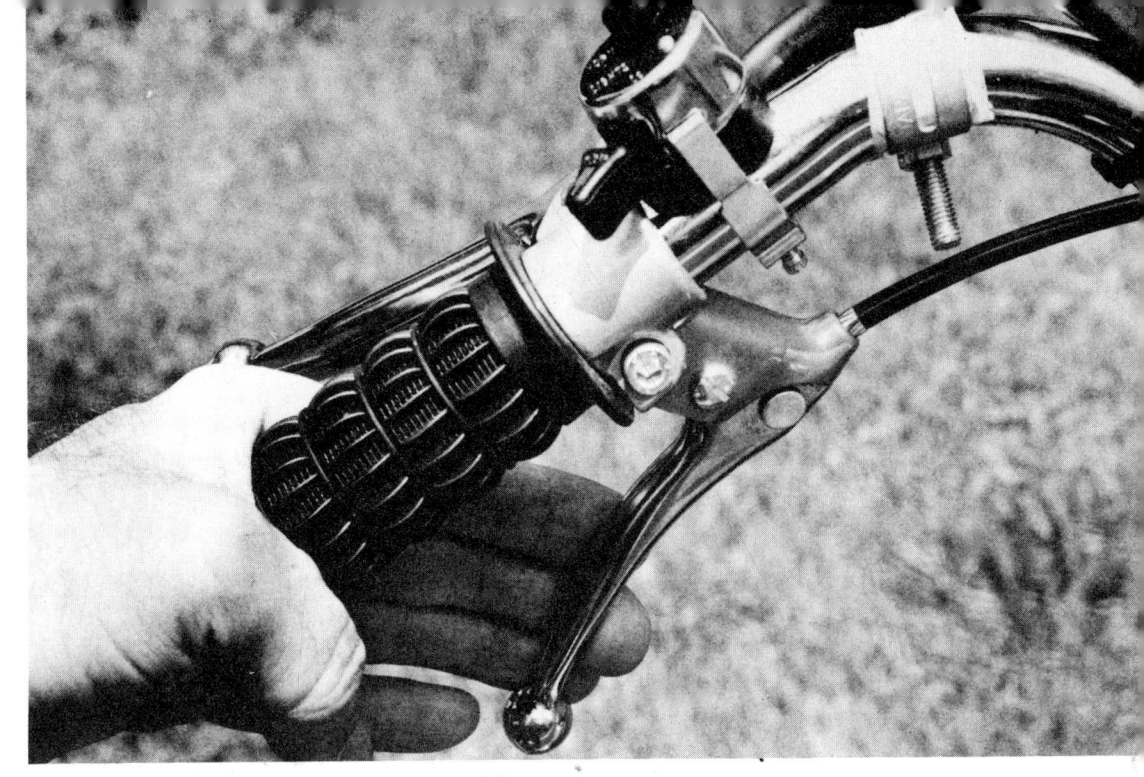

On a moped, the clutch levers are under the lefthand brake lever, as shown. To stop the engine, use the ignition switch, not the clutch lever!

Normally the pedal of a moped is used to kick-start the 50cc engine, except that the direction of the kick is forward, as when pedaling.

To stop a scooter or motorcycle engine, simply turn off the ignition. In both instances, don't forget to close the fuel line valve.

Warning: Never let an engine idle too long. It will overheat.

EXHAUST PIPES

When you buy a machine, the exhaust muffling system (silencers) fitted to the engine meets the requirements of the law. Don't change it into something that makes a lot of noise but does not in reality produce any increase in power.

Some riders argue, "It sounds good. Everybody turns to look when I pass." Don't be so sure they're admiring you. In most cases they're saying, "Listen to that jerk," and they're hoping the police show up with the appropriate summons. The nuisance of the noise is far greater than any possible benefit. One racing expert summed it up this way: "A machine used for racing has to breathe much harder than a street bike, so we use pipes that do the job best. The noise is there; but it's contained at the track, and the people accept it as part of the scene. But that kind of noise in city streets and on country roads is downright stupid. Anyone who alters the pipes in order to produce a loud exhaust sound, to attract attention, to feel special or important, is really showing her- or himself up for a fool. Cops should stop them, and they should be made to obey the law. For my money there's nothing more impressive than seeing a two-wheeler gliding along—powerful, smooth, silent. You can't help looking twice to admire the machine and the rider."

YOUR OPERATIONS LOG

It's a good idea to keep a running log or record of what happened to your two-wheeler and what maintenance you've performed on the various parts. A glance will then tell you many facts about its condition and remind you of things that need to be done. A good log will remind you to change oil, oil the chain, check the brake linings, adjust the clutch and brake cables, and of many other things that normally escape attention.

Your owner's handbook will have a list of services that should be performed at regular intervals, and you can use that list with your own log as a reminder and a record.

Remember that any system of maintenance is better than no system at all. You've invested in a machine, so invest a little time in recording what's happening to it.

LONG-TERM STORAGE

Many riders hang up their helmets for the winter months and store their machines somewhere to wait for better weather. But if the machine is stored improperly, it can end up in a damaged state. Dampness is the worst enemy, so always try to put your bike in a dry area, and set up the machine as follows:

The best way to store a *bicycle* is to set it upside down on its seat and handlebar or simply to hang it up by its frame (*not* its wheel rims). Use hooks that will not scratch the paint on the frame. Before you store it away, whether it's a bicycle or motorized machine, first clean off all the accumulated dirt; then polish the chromed and painted surfaces. Let some air out of the tires, and apply a light coat of oil to the chain and sprockets.

Storing *mopeds, scooters, and motorcycles* needs a little more care. First warm up the engine by idling it a short time; then drain the crankcase oil (not on a two-stroke engine) into a clean container. You cannot use this oil back in the engine, but you can use it on the chain, cables, etc. (if it's not so far gone that it should be thrown out).

Remove the spark plug of each cylinder, pour about two ounces of clean oil into the cylinder, and turn the engine over several times with the kick starter so the oil is spread along the cylinder wall. Replace the spark plug, finger tight, and leave it that way.

Disconnect and remove the battery from the machine, and store it in the basement or a heated garage, where, from time to time, you can hook a trickle charger to it for a day or two in order to keep the battery in a charged state. You'll appreciate a good battery when you hook it up again come spring. Periodically check the electrolyte level, and add distilled water to keep the plates covered.

Set the machine itself on its center stand and prop up the rear and front forks with a piece of wood, in order to keep both wheels off the ground. Let some air out of the tires. Apply a little oil to the chain and drive sprockets.

"Just a minute," you may object. "Why go through all that when you can make it easy on yourself by starting up the engine once every week? It'll even keep the battery charged."

Many beginners like this approach simply because they lack experience or may be too lazy to do it the right way. Starting up the engine for a short warm-up period and then shutting it off simply produces a lot of condensation inside the engine, which is very harmful.

When the warmer weather arrives and your urge to ride is awakened, be sure to pump up the tires to the correct pressures and, in the case of motorized machines, connect the battery to the correct wires. Fill the crankcase with the right amount of correct engine oil, tighten the spark plug, and connect its wire. Start up the engine, and check the clutch and brake levers for proper operation.

Despite your precautions, the engine may still not start up. The following is a more detailed troubleshooting guide which you may want to use, along with the suggestions in your owner's handbook.

TROUBLE AND CAUSE GUIDE

1. **Engine cannot be cranked.**
   This may be caused by a broken piston ring, or the piston may be seized because of lack of lubrication. You may also have a broken crankshaft. Either way, the engine has to be opened for major work.

2. **Engine can be cranked but will not start.**
   These negative fuel conditions may exist: Clogged vent cap. Empty fuel tank. Fuel valve closed. Fuel too old. Fuel line, filter, or carb clogged. Defective carb gasket.
   Then check if these spark conditions exist: Ignition switch not on. Incorrect or fouled plug. Cable to plug loose, or disconnected.

Plug gap incorrect. Defective transistor unit. Defective crankcase gasket (on two-stroker). Blown fuse. Dead battery.

3. **Engine starts, then stops.**
   Possible causes: Wrong adjustment of fuel and air (usually too lean). Choke closed. On two-stroker, wrong mixture of gas and oil. Spark plug fouled, or wrong type. Water in fuel. Fuel too old. Punctured float. Loose wiring. Defective crankcase gasket (on two-stroker).
   Make same checks as in paragraph 2.

4. **Engine runs poorly.**
   Possible causes: Overheated engine or plug. Wrong type of plug. Damaged plug. Spark advanced too far. Possible buildup of carbon in cylinder head, around exhaust port, or in muffler system.
   Make same checks as in paragraph 3.

5. **Engine loses power.**
   Possible causes: Too much carbon in cylinder head or muffler system. Partially clogged fuel line or filters. Ignition advance or carb set incorrectly. Piston ring damaged. Cylinder badly worn. Throttle slide or cable sticking. Defective gaskets at crankcase, head, or carb. Brake shoes dragging.

6. **Machine rides but is jerky.**
   Possible causes: Dirty clutch jaws. Damage of a mechanical part.

Take the time to study the owner's handbook that came with your machine. You'll never appreciate it more than when you get stuck on the road and one of its special pointers helps you get rolling again.

You— the Rider

4

All kinds of people are handling vehicles, and soon you'll be among them. Drivers can be good, bad, meek, belligerent, careless, overcautious, indifferent, road hogs, showoffs, and every other kind you can think up. On your two-wheeler you will have to cope with the way these people behave in traffic. You will have to exist with them, yet protect yourself from them.

All drivers handle themselves in traffic in a way that they believe is right, but that may actually be incompetent or unacceptable to others. Every person's attitude toward traffic situations is different, and very few people will admit their faults or realize that they are unprepared to be in traffic.

Here are some overheard examples of defensive reactions:

"Are you gonna tell me how to drive? I've been driving for over thirty years! I don't need your advice, and besides, if you'd been in your lane, I wouldn't have hit you!"

"Okay. I admit I was above the speed limit, but he should've looked both ways before he came out of his driveway."

"I was very careful, Officer. I was in my lane, with my directional signals on. Then he came out of nowhere from the side and hit me. It wasn't my fault. I was watching the car in front of me."

"So I went through the red light. Do you have to give me a ticket? There were no cars around. Come on, have a heart. I didn't do anything wrong."

"I was driving along, and the next thing . . . well, I don't know.

The road was clear, and I didn't see a thing. All of a sudden there was the car in front of me, but I just don't know how it happened."

"I saw the stop sign, and I started to use my brakes. But it was his fault. I'm telling you—I just didn't have a chance to use them."

These are just a few of the kinds of people out there. Each is right, and each is never going to admit a fault. Attitudes that cause us to act and react are the controlling force behind the things we do.

Some attitudes can keep you safe in traffic, while others can get you into an accident. They affect your riding and personal survival, regardless of the kind of traffic or drivers you may confront. The sooner you realize both your positive and negative traits, the sooner you'll become a better rider and driver. A traffic accident situation does not create itself—operators of vehicles do.

If more vehicle operators used this view as a guide, and if driving schools stressed it as the all-important factor, then our national highway accident rate might be lowered greatly.

Consider a brief list of positive and negative attitudes, and then reason out for yourself how these could create the situations that lead to a crash.

Positive

Confidence in personal ability
Respect for the rights of others
Pride
Courtesy toward others
Alertness and quick reflexes
Defensive caution
Technical knowledge
Knowing the value of traffic
    rules

Negative

Overconfidence
Impatience

Arrogance
A quick temper
Indifference
Carelessness
Exhibitionism
Belligerence

How often have you seen a *belligerent* person ignore a stop sign or red light? How often have you seen a *defiant* person drive the wrong way on a one-way street or road? A *slowpoke* or an *indifferent* driver may create a traffic jam in which the *impatient* one may cause an accident by simply not wanting to wait like the rest. A *road bully* may crowd you aside, unexpectedly, and right into a ditch. The *arrogant* one may speed by you with only an inch to spare from being forced into the path of a truck. A *neglectful* one may not have checked the brakes in a long time and now finds he or she can't stop from slamming into you.

What safety experts and psychologists are advocating is that we all must accept the traffic environment for what it is and must look for better and more foolproof ways to exist in it. The only controllable factor is in the traits and attitudes of those who handle vehicles.

One night, as I was driving home in my car, I approached an intersection where the green light gave me the right-of-way. A young rider on a moped came into view from the right side street. It was obvious that he was not going to stop for the red light on his side. While he must have known that a moped must obey all traffic rules, to his way of thinking the red light could hardly be meant for a small machine. Many bicycle riders feel and act the same way.

The following afternoon at that same corner another young rider on a powerful dirt machine came roaring up the one-way street, trying to outrun the police car behind him. He was riding his unlicensed bike home rather than pushing it from the bay area where many others race around and practice in the dirt. In trying to outrun the police, he ran into a car, and his machine ended up a twisted heap, while he ended up with his leg broken.

Imagine yourself barreling along on your motorcycle at night on an unfamiliar road. As you approach a fairly tight curve, you don't bother easing off, and you then find a car backing fast out of a hidden driveway. Screech ... crash! As you pick yourself up, examine your crushed bike, and angrily exchange registration information, you should admit, at least to yourself, that you've been riding with a careless attitude. You couldn't see around that curve, yet you were smug in your conviction that no car at that exact moment would be backing out of a hidden driveway. Thus, your attitude got you into that accident.

When you leave your 10-speed bicycle unchained and unguarded on some street and later find your bike has disappeared, you realize you're a trusting soul who has faith in people, but your admirable attitude was, in this case, misdirected.

The younger you are, the more trusting you are likely to be because you don't yet have "bitter experience." Apply it to traffic, and you'll quickly appreciate the fact that there's no substitute for experience. Older riders have a healthy respect for the unseen dangers that lurk at every corner and on the straightaways, and they've also learned a long time ago that you must *never* depend on how others in traffic will react to any given situation. After you experience a few tricky traffic situations you'll have stories to tell, based on bitter experience.

Pete gets on his bicycle and starts down the winding road to visit his friend Joe, but in the meantime, Joe is doing the same thing, coming toward Pete. They meet, right where the road straightens out, and they start circling each other, talking. A common scene. Now a car comes along, and the driver slows down. Just as the car is alongside Pete and Joe, the driver speeds up, and Pete goes into a sharp lean. The driver swerves, misses Pete, but hits Joe. While Joe wasn't hurt badly, the point is that the accident should not have happened. The two bike riders should not have been riding in circles when they saw the car approaching, and the driver would have done better by stopping rather than swerving.

The car driver felt secure in his position and did not expect a sudden change in direction by Pete, and both Pete and Joe felt secure in their familiar neighborhood. *The feeling of security always exists for a few moments just before something unexpected happens,* and statistics point out that most accidents take place very close to home—where everything is familiar and secure.

One sunny day, George was breezing along on his 450 cc on a two-lane highway, approaching a smaller road feeding in from the right side from the valley below. The roads were separated by some trees and bushes. The feed-in road was clearly visible from the highway. Traffic was light in both directions, with only one car in the slow lane in front of George. As George and the car approached the feed-in road, another car came up it, toward the stop sign. The driver of the car in front of George thought the other car, coming uphill, was not going to stop, so he edged toward the left lane to protect himself. But just then George had decided to pass the car in front of him and was pouring on power, and he was then caught in a squeeze as he saw a car bearing down on him from the opposite direction. George cut across the road and put his machine into a slide to stop himself from flying into a ditch. He was badly hurt. He blamed the driver of the car in front of him for forcing him out.

Whom would you blame? Can you point out the attitudes?

The driver on the feed-in road obeyed the stop sign although he came up rather fast. The driver in front of George was exercising caution and by instinct moved toward the left (without looking), thus forcing George into a tight spot. George should have known that whenever you put yourself alongside a car, you should be sure to have an escape route.

Whether you're starting out as a new rider or have had some experience on a two-wheeler, a brief look at specific attitudes will come in handy.

CONFIDENCE

When you know the technical points of your machine, what you're supposed to do in whatever traffic situation exists, and how to handle your machine, then you're confident, and nothing is going to shake you out of it.

OVERCONFIDENCE

Imagine an attitude of overconfidence meeting up with an attitude of impatience. You're on your two-wheeler and coming up to an intersection where the light has just switched from green to amber. "I can make it before it turns red," you think as you add speed to the situation. The car driver on your right is impatiently waiting out his red light, and when he sees the flicker of amber intended for you, he knows he'll have to go-ahead green in another second. But why wait? He takes off before the green, and you're caught in the intersection on the red. Some bad accidents happen this way, and as the crowd gathers around the mess, you swear too late that you'll never again try to beat the red light.

My friend Rick learned the hard way about overconfidence. He used to amaze me the way he would lean into curves, in spite of the balding old tires on his thumper, but one day he discovered the relationship between tire traction and overconfidence. Luckily there were good car drivers alongside and in back of him when he fell and began sliding. His attitude of overconfidence cost him a broken kick starter, a twisted handlebar, a ripped tank, shredded clothing, and an injured knee. That experience slowed him down for a time, until he bought new tires, when overconfidence returned in full glory! He has since misjudged the stopping power of his brakes (smacked into the rear of a car), misjudged his ability to shift fast (missed a gear and couldn't get out of the way of the taxi that knocked him over), and has even misjudged his endurance for long-distance riding (dozed off during a night ride and left the road). Soon he'll be a very unhappy rider—his license will be suspended.

It's good to have confidence, but overconfidence can be quite dangerous.

TIMIDITY, FEAR, AND CAUTION

A timid or meek person may lack courage, but many timid people have performed some exceptionally daring and courageous acts. The timid and the meek are expressing *caution,* and they take only calculated risks. Behind it is always a specific reason.

Here an overconfident rider is trailing a car too closely at 55 mph. For your own safety, keep a sensible amount of space in front of you.

This bicycle rider feels he has the right to go against the traffic. Neither car drivers nor pedestrians expect this, which creates many accidents.

"Ever since I rode my bicycle into that tunnellike underpass and the bus thundered past me with only inches to spare, I've been afraid to ride. And you know how I used to love bicycling."

"Did you stop riding right then and there?"

"No. I rode my bike home. But I can't forget that awful feeling of being trapped in that tunnel. Now I'm simply afraid to ride."

"Maybe your problem is in your imagination. You keep visualizing that bus in that dark tunnel. In fact, you rode your bike home without any trouble, and that indicates something positive. When you think back, what comes to mind?"

"Oh, God! I see myself lying there in the gutter, crushed to death under those big wheels."

"But the fact is it didn't happen the way you insist on visualizing it. You rode a straight line through the tunnel, which was the right thing to do, and so did the bus. And nothing happened. You're reliving that incident, injecting a 'fear condition' into it. The result is, you're building up a real fear inside yourself. What happened has actually made you into a better bike rider."

"Are you kidding?"

"Seriously. From now on you'll be much more aware of other dangerous situations. You'll be watching for hidden threats. You'll avoid anything that appears dangerous. You'll know bad situations can be created, but you won't let them take place. Stop seeing yourself crushed under bus wheels when nothing of the sort is happening. *Stop imagining bad situations.*"

The outcome in this case was a good one. Fear of riding in traffic is natural, but it can be eliminated through a proper approach. The most often heard complaint is: "I'm afraid I won't know what to do if I have to stop fast." That simply means that there's serious need for more practice in handling the machine.

"I get scared when cars come too close to me." Any rider will get scared, but the experienced ones will do their best to keep away from tight situations. It's so easy to let them pass by and leave all the space for you.

"I'm always afraid car drivers won't see me." There are many lazy, indifferent, and careless drivers who have no trouble seeing whatever interests them on sidewalks but can't see a two-wheeler in front of them. Make it easier on yourself by *wearing bright-colored clothing and helmet,* and practice glancing to the rear to be sure of what's following you.

"Intersections scare me—I'm never sure when it's safe to go." If you have to cross an intersection, remember that cars may cut you off, whether you're obeying the law or riding blindly into a squeeze. All intersections have control signs or lights, but *cross only when it's absolutely safe.* Even if you have to wait a few minutes.

Fear feeds on itself. The more you think and imagine traffic dangers, the more real they become in your mind. Try the opposite tack: Think and imagine in positive terms! Spend a lot of time practicing on your machine so that you can handle it automatically, without having to look for the controls. Practice your figure eights, sharp turns, and panic stops.

It's important to be cautious when riding in traffic, but avoid being overcautious to the degree that you're actually hesitant or undecided. This can create a dangerous situation. Check yourself. Are you going too slowly for the lane you're in? Are cars passing you on your right? Do you slow down too much at corners? Do you take more time to do something than is considered normal time (like feeding into a road)?

In these situations some car drivers may become impatient with you, and your slowness may cause them to make a wrong move. Take the time to practice where the traffic is light and where no one will bother you. Build up enough confidence so you won't hesitate to move into the flow of traffic, rather than jam it up.

PRIDE

My friend Valerie rides a moped but to watch her, you'd think she was sitting on a $5,000 European import and daring you to keep up with her. Top speed on her moped is 20, yet she seems to be sailing along much faster, and enjoying it. She keeps that moped in spotless condition and is constantly checking out every nut and bolt. And never a problem in starting the engine—one kick to prime; switch on; then kick and go! After any run, her engine is shut down with deliberate care, the machine then set up on its stand in one safe corner of the garage. When she rides she has self-confidence and determination, and she's quick to notice every change in the traffic pattern far ahead and conducts herself accordingly. Never a need to panic, never an indecision, never any attempt to force the machine to exceed its performance capabilities.

One day I complimented her and ended by saying "You always do the right thing, and you never get excited or confused. It's a pleasure to watch you."

"It's a pleasure to ride," she said.

"Ever have an accident?"

"No, of course not."

"It could happen."

She thought it over. "I suppose so, but I'm going to continue being careful. If anything happened, I'd be mortified. I'd be so ashamed! That's one reason I'm so careful. If I had an accident, my moped would get all dented and scratched. I'd be very unhappy, so I take no chances."

Pride in self and in machine. You ride a certain way because you want to preserve a good image of yourself. My friend, being young and adventurous, eventually sold her moped to a girlfriend and then bought a 350 cc motorcycle! She keeps that machine in tiptop condition, and when she's in traffic, she handles herself just like a pro.

THE THRILL SEEKERS

There are thrills one can handle, and there are those that can send you to the hospital. If you like to tear around on your motorcycle over rough ground, then you can have fun by getting into competition motocross, dirt track, and other racing. But don't look for thrills while riding in traffic!

A very good friend was boasting to me how he likes to ride his bicycle in heavy traffic, cutting in and out between cars and people.

When I said I didn't think he was being too smart, his reply was: "Why not? It's a lot of fun."

"What if you smacked into a car and got hurt? You don't even wear a helmet to protect your head," I pointed out.

"It's my head. I'm the one who's getting hurt if anything happens."

"Well," I said, "you're thinking only about the kicks you're getting out of that kind of riding. You're part of the group who resent having to wear helmets, saying you have the right to do whatever you want. But you're not thinking of your family. If you're hurt badly, they're the ones who will have the burden of caring for you. You could be out of the scene for a long time, and that means you're not thinking about your future. And the driver of the car you hit will end up with a stiffer charge against him than if it was just a matter of bruised elbows and skinned knuckles."

For the thrill that lasts one or five seconds, you could hurt yourself, and others, in a way that could last for years. Looking for thrills in regular street and road traffic is nothing more than being a thoughtless exhibitionist, pleasing only yourself. If thrills are what you want, then take your urge—which will have to be backed up with a lot of skill and determination—to the races where everything is conducted by rules of safety. There every rider in a competition is taking only a calculated risk. But don't take risks in regular traffic.

ARROGANCE, BELLIGERENCE, AND CARELESSNESS

Have you ever met the arrogant rider who brags about the many times he or she has beaten a stoplight or outraced somebody to the next corner? Or seen a grinning rider weaving in and out of lanes without bothering to signal or even turn his head to make sure he's clear? Or watched the rider who brakes hard for every stop and then screeches away wide open?

These same riders howl with indignation when something happens to them as a result of their own negative attitudes. By law, bicycles and mopeds must be on the far right side of the roadway, except when preparing for a left turn.

INDIFFERENCE AND LAZINESS

"One of my brakes isn't holding too well. I know I should adjust it, but it'll have to wait until I have more time."

When will you have more time? While mending your bones after the accident? Nothing on your two-wheeler will adjust itself, and you'll discover this when you suddenly need a lot of brake power in an emergency.

Have you ever been out riding with your friends single file and come up to an intersection where the lead rider ignored the stop or yield sign and crossed through without even glancing to the sides to see if the way was safe? And the whole group, including you, followed him? You may not want to tag your leader as lazy because it doesn't take much effort to glance around, but it certainly takes an indifferent person to ignore what could possibly happen in such a situation.

Any intersection in which traffic is moving is a dangerous place and needs all the attention you can give it! This is where accidents happen to lazy and indifferent people, as well as overconfident ones and arrogant thrill seekers.

THE MACHO RIDER

There is a small group of riders with the attitude that they belong to the tough clan or clique; they ride and dress to create an image of toughness and to attract attention. When these negative attitudes are used by riders in traffic, they create a poor image for the thousands of other riders who display positive attitudes. If you're willing to give honest answers to some basic questions, you'll discover where your own attitudes place you.

Do you respect the rights of others? Don't say yes if you like to cut others off at corners or crowd them out of lanes. Showing respect for the rights of others does not make you a weakling. It takes solid willpower to admit you're wrong, to let your brain rather than your quick emotions control you.

Do you like to take chances? Don't say no if you enjoy clipping close to car fenders, coming to fast stops, roaring away from every light, or speeding through intersections.

Do you always turn your head to check the traffic behind you before making lane changes or turns? Don't say yes if you ride with your eyes fixed only twenty feet ahead of your front wheel and believe that everybody else sees you and knows what your next move will be. You can tell a good rider by the way he or she constantly swivels to see what's alongside or behind.

Are you too lazy or forgetful to signal your intentions? Don't expect others to guess what you'll do next. And signal *before* you act—at least a block before reaching the corner, at least 100 feet before turning off a highway.

Do you fit your riding to the existing traffic flow? Not if you speed in crowded places, crawl along when the rest are cruising at 50, take too long to make up your mind about turning, or forget which road you're supposed to use when you reach the fork.

Can you, without looking, put your hand on every control? Fumbling for things while riding can get you into trouble. It shows you haven't mastered your machine yet. For your own benefit, spend more time riding in an empty lot, and get really acquainted.

Are you able to ride and at the same time read a map, tighten a bolt, fix a loose wire connection, adjust the carb, or admire the scenery? Don't say yes, because it's nothing to brag about. If you need to do anything other than ride, pull over and stop in a safe area. Riding is a full-time job!

Are you constantly alert to what's going on around you and way up ahead of you? You should be, because if you lose track of the situation, you could become disoriented at a moment when you need all your concentration. Alertness is one attitude that will always keep you safe.

Are you a good judge of speed and distance? You should be because when you're moving at top speed, you need enough space to keep out of harm.

Are you quick to notice changes in the traffic pattern ahead of you? The more you notice, the safer you'll be.

Are you by nature slow to react? Even at 10 mph, a quick response on your part will get you out of a bad situation. Think how much swifter your reaction must be at 50 mph. If you're unalert, absentminded, or sluggish, you'll increase your chances of having an accident.

Have you ever had a close call or been in an accident? If so, then you have something to think about and analyze in order to put the blame where it rightly belongs. And remember, it takes courage to admit you're wrong, but such acceptance is the best teacher for your future.

These two riders are aware of the heavy traffic around them as they weave through the tight lanes. Their cautious attitude will help ensure their survival.

Physics tells us that when vehicles crash, the meeting of opposed forces causes things to be damaged and fly in all directions. This law applies to both machinery and human bodies. Drivers and passengers of automobiles are better protected than riders on two-wheelers, and for this reason you need to understand better when and why that law of physics applies to you.

TIRE TRACTION AND MOMENTUM

These could be friends or foes, depending on how they're used or abused.

"Oh, no! Look at those tire skid marks! That must have been a terrible accident!"

It was, and it left three persons mangled beyond recognition, even though they were somewhat protected by the steel bodies of the cars. The tire skid marks showed that one of the drivers slammed on his power brakes in an attempt to stop. The wheels locked, and locked wheels produce only screeching and skids. Bear in mind that *tires cannot bring a vehicle to a controlled stop when momentum exceeds the limit of tire traction.* Any skid, short or long, is the result of momentum (speed), vehicle weight, and the road surface.

Whether you're moving at a slow 20 or cruising at 50, you'll have a feeling of security as long as nothing interferes with you. If a stiff wind were to hit you suddenly from the side, you would lose that feeling. Increase that wind to strong gusts, and you could even panic on your two-wheeler. All your security rests on the tires of your machine.

Suppose that a two-wheeler were going through a curve at average speed, with an easy lean to the right. At this speed the tires have no trouble keeping you safe. Now increase your speed (pedal faster, or open the throttle slightly). If you now wanted to tighten the curve, you would have to lean harder. At this point your tires would still be holding the road surface. The more you lean, the more you tighten the line of the curve, and the faster you must go if you want the tires to hold. Your momentum, in the form of centrifugal force, wants to carry you outside the curved line, and if you tighten the line even

In a sudden emergency you may need to kill the engine, so be sure you know where the switch is, shown here at right thumb.

more, you'll have to lean still harder. And at that point tire traction or adhesion is lost! Your machine slides out, and if your tires could talk, they'd say, "How much does the fool think I can take?" On a wet surface you'll slide out even sooner.

If you analyze the meaning of "lost control" in the majority of accident reports, you'll see the law of physics operating: momentum and lack of tire adhesion playing their parts. Speed is a force in motion. Tire traction or adhesion is a holding force. There's a limit to what these can do, and if you exceed the limits, you end up in trouble. And in every instance of trouble, *your attitude put you there.*

You must now devote some time to learning how to handle your two-wheeler in a safe practice area where nobody will bother you. Try to develop automatic reactions to every kind of riding situation so that you'll handle your machine with full confidence when you go out into traffic.

If everyone made sure his or her vehicle was in good working condition, learned to handle that vehicle properly under both normal and emergency conditions, admitted that *bad attitudes* can create traffic hazards, remained alert at all times, and obeyed all traffic rules—then we would have NO ACCIDENTS!

Your Survival in Traffic

5

Stand on any corner in any town or city and watch two-wheelers go by. Watch how the rider handles the machine. Smoothly or jerkily? Does the rider look around constantly or never bother? Watch how he comes to stops and how he starts off. And from all this even a novice can predict how that rider will fare in the long run.

From the positive point of view, two-wheelers are highly maneuverable machines and can easily get out of the way of harm—when they're handled by experienced riders. While bicycles and mopeds are capable of quick turns and fast stops but are not capable of quick bursts of speed, they are nevertheless able to keep out of dangerous situations. Scooters and motorcycles pose no problems insofar as performance is concerned (in capable hands); these machines can be very nimble in traffic and have excellent handling characteristics and stopping power.

Two-wheelers are safe vehicles for fun and for transportation but are only as safe as the rider on them.

Any two-wheeler is very vulnerable, and the rider and passenger are constantly exposed to a possible spill and even a bad crash. In most collisions a car will remain upright on its four wheels with the occupants well protected inside. A two-wheeler in the same collision will end up all over the road, with the riders badly hurt.

It would be impossible to simplify traffic problems into one nutshell rule because it's impossible to relate every human attitude to every traffic situation. But one can imagine some possible situations, and from these you can develop an awareness of what can happen. It will be your attitude that will get you into, or keep you out of, bad traffic situations.

Fix in your mind what traffic really is. Imagine yourself watching traffic from a high vantage point, and notice that all sorts of vehicles flow in a stream, moving in one direction, some turning here, others there, and sometimes all slowing down and coming to a stop so other traffic from side streets can feed in or cross their path. The job of every vehicle operator is to *keep moving with the flow of traffic and not disrupt it* by slowing down needlessly or making abrupt turns without signaling. All that traffic can be safe and without incidents only when the drivers and riders are constantly aware of conditions far enough in advance so that nobody is surprised, thus creating a suddenly dangerous situation. The more aware you are of changes in the traffic pattern, the safer you'll be!

Practice riding your two-wheeler until you can handle it as naturally as you breathe or walk. Soon you'll develop the required skill and will ride naturally and automatically. *If you can't control your two-wheeler expertly in a practice area, you certainly won't be able to do so in traffic. Always ride with the proper attitude toward others,* and suppress and control your own negative feelings which can lead you into trouble.

Many people believe that anybody can ride a bicycle and that riding a moped is even easier. But this kind of attitude usually puts riders into trouble, sooner or later. Too many bicyclists imagine themselves to be safe on so simple a machine and are then shocked when they find themselves involved in an accident. Handling even a bicycle in traffic must be taken seriously. Young bicycle riders may be very good riders in a protected area, but too many meet with disaster when they enter street and road traffic. When you're in control of your machine and aware of the traffic, riding is a pleasure, but when you're not at ease or unsure of what to expect, then riding can be torture.

"But I'm new at this," you say, "and I can't help being scared."

Naturally. And that's a good way to start. It shows that you want to prepare yourself properly in order to be able to handle the unknown. Some beginning riders think that a few runs around the block are all the practice they need. By some miracle, this is often the only experience they have when they go for (and pass) their riding test. The fact remains that their experience is too limited for what they'll meet in the long run. If they're very careful, they might even survive, but what you want is more than such meager ability.

The first question is: "Can you ride a bicycle?"

Panic! "I've never handled any kind of a two-wheeler. Not even a bicycle! Does that leave me out?"

Not at all. Start off on a bicycle in a simple, easy way called the downhill coasting method. With this method you don't even need anyone to hold you up while you're learning. You can do it all yourself, with excellent results. The method should be used with a motorized machine as well.

Your first step is to find a smooth downhill path or road on which cars seldom travel. The grade shouldn't be too steep, nothing more than an incline, just enough to keep you rolling slowly downhill. You won't be trying to build up speed. On a bicycle (for these practice lessons only), lower the seat so your feet can reach the ground when you're seated. Keep your feet on the ground and your hands on the handlebar grips, and push yourself forward about five or so feet. Then squeeze the brake levers to test the brakes. On a scooter or motorcycle you'll have only one right-hand brake lever to work. You now have the feel of the machine's weight, and you know the brakes are working. A scooter or motorcycle may at first feel heavy, but as the machine starts to roll, the weight will disappear.

Use your feet to push yourself and start rolling slowly downhill. Use them to balance yourself at the beginning; then keep them from touching the ground, and let the machine roll forward. As you begin building up speed, use the brakes to slow down. If you've had enough, stop and rest.

If rolling downhill comes easily and naturally to you, try weaving from side to side. Use your body to lean, and the machine will follow you into a curve. At slow speeds you'll have to point the front wheel in the direction you want to go, but at higher speeds you simply lean. Don't overdo the lean, and don't use the brakes when you're in a curve! If you're on a scooter or motorcycle, start using the foot brake as your speed builds up, and if the downgrade is fairly long, practice using both brakes, front and rear, at the same time. Develop the habit of using both brakes in all situations.

Your second step with a bicycle will be to pedal on level ground, and for this practice you should first raise the seat to the proper height so that your pedaling leg will be nearly straight on the downstroke. Use the lowest gear to start rolling, and in the beginning stay in that low gear as you pedal around an empty lot to improve your skill and build up your confidence. Again, don't try for speed. Try for control!

After you feel confident that you can handle your bicycle, practice changing gears as you travel in a straight line. Using easy strokes on the pedals, move the gearshift lever forward to the next highest gear (or position marked 2 or N on a 3-speed model). Remember that on a derailleur (5- and 10-speed models) you must be pedaling while changing gears! Shifting is done by *feel*—move the lever slightly, and after the chain has shifted to the next sprocket, see if you can eliminate the grinding or clanking sound, if any, by moving the shift lever a small amount backward or forward.

A moped will be even easier in this level ground practice after you have rolled downhill a few times and got the feel of the machine. First set the machine on its center stand, and start up the engine; then, keeping your hands on the brake levers and being ready to use the brakes if you have to, push the machine off the stand and get on. Let go of the brake levers. If your moped begins moving (creeping forward), it means the idling speed of the engine is set too fast and should be slowed down (to prevent burning the clutch plates). Switch on the lights. To move forward, simply speed up the engine a bit by turning the throttle twistgrip toward you, counterclockwise. Don't start speeding, especially not if you're on a brand-new machine. Keep the speed to around 10 mph. To slow down or come to a stop, shut off the throttle by turning it away from you, clockwise, and use the hand brake levers, with an easy and even squeezing force. That's all you can do with a moped, but that little will give you a lot of fun out in the fresh air and will serve as a practical means of transportation.

On a scooter or motorcycle, your second step is a different practice because now you'll have to learn how to use the throttle, clutch, and gearshift lever. First, start up the engine, leave the gears in *neutral* so that you don't have to worry about the clutch and the gearshift lever, and, as you did before, simply roll downhill several times, using the brakes to slow down and zigzagging to get the feel of the machine. Secondly, do the same thing, except this time play the throttle a few times as you're rolling along. The engine is not pulling you, of course. You'll need a good buddy to help push the machine back uphill to the starting line after each downhill coasting run.

Build up your confidence before you go on to the next step. It's not unusual for a good bicyclist to become scared when he or she mounts a motorized machine and hears the engine running. Having to add the clutching and shifting can easily add to the confusion.

Your third step (on a scooter or motorcycle) is to use the clutch and gears. With the engine running at the starting line, squeeze the clutch lever all the way, and with your left foot shift into first gear. The shifting pattern on all new motorcycles is *down once for first gear* and then *up* for the rest. Bear in mind that some scooters and older motorcycles could have a different shift pattern! Now foot-push yourself into coasting position, all the while holding the clutch lever squeezed (clutch disengaged). As you start rolling downhill, get your feet onto the pegs or footrests of the scooter, and slowly release (engage) the clutch. Do *not* open the throttle more than a crack—just enough to increase your speed a bit. Remember that in first gear you have a lot of power, so any sudden opening of the throttle can send you flying.

Halfway downhill squeeze the clutch (disengage), and shut off power. Use the foot brake to come to a full stop. Now shift into neutral as you still hold the clutch. If your machine has a light to indicate when you're in neutral, check it as you lift the shift lever *once* with your toes. If you have no light on your model machine, then you'll have to feel for the neutral position. When you think you're in it, *slowly* start releasing the clutch lever, and if the machine doesn't creep forward, you've got it. If the machine starts to move, squeeze the clutch fully, and try again for that neutral gear position. Practice does it.

Your fourth and final step. For this practice you should take your machine to a legally designated practice area where no one will interfere with you. The area should be flat and without obstructions; there are many deserted roads, parking lots, or fields that will serve your purpose. Wear your helmet and goggles, full shoes or boots, gloves, and suitable clothing to protect your body.

You'll now practice shifting gears from low on up until it becomes automatic in every way, whether you're moving straight, going in circles, or making figure eights. Soon you won't have to look for the shift lever, wonder which gear you're in, or be afraid that you've forgotten where the brakes are. Practice stopping smoothly, then stopping fast. Practice slowing down through the gears, almost coming to a full stop, and, without putting down your feet, starting up again in first gear, and shifting to second, third, then slowing down again by shifting down to second, and then first, and still not touching the ground with your feet again start up through the gears.

Find out just how fast you can stop, without spilling, of course. If you're doing only 25 mph on a dry road, you'll need about twenty-five feet in which to stop, using both brakes. If your reflexes are quick, you might shorten the stopping distance (some disc brakes will stop you quicker, in a shorter distance). *Do not* use your brakes when cornering! Practice using both brakes together.

You'll need even more practice before you try tangling with traffic. You don't really have any significant experience at this stage. So let's take up a few of the finer points that relate to expert riding.

Sit properly. When you're riding your two-wheeler, you should feel comfortable, and comfort starts with proper posture. A hunched-forward position will tire your shoulders and eventually your whole body. So will the habit of gripping the handlebar with all your might. Sit upright, and relax your waist. Hold the grips lightly so the vibrations from the front fork don't give you muscle tension and a headache. On a bicycle, moped, and scooter, keep your knees parallel with the center line of the machine. On a motorcycle, keep your knees against the rubber pads on the sides of the gas tank. While riding, form the habit of turning your head all the time to see what's behind you and at your sides, and also keep a sharp lookout far ahead so that nothing in the traffic ahead will surprise you. Whenever you're on rough roads or see a rut or pothole which you can't possibly avoid, stand up on the pegs (footrests) in order to lower the center of gravity. Bicycles and mopeds don't have the suspension systems for taking rough surfaces, and for this reason you must look far ahead to avoid trouble. Even a shallow pothole can dump a speeding bicycle or moped rider.

Throttle and clutch. It's important that your hands rest properly on the handlebar grips. In all cases, your hold should be easy and firm, but not a do-or-die hold. Experienced motorcycle riders have a way of holding the throttle from *underneath,* without the wrist's being cocked over the top of the twistgrip. In this way, if a sudden shock (hitting a hole or rock unexpectedly) snaps them backward on the seat, the underhanded hold on the throttle will serve only to shut off power. With the wrist cocked over the throttle, power would be turned on, and control lost. On scooters and motorcycles, rest one or two fingers of your left hand on the clutch lever, just in case you need to pull it quickly.

Concentrate. When you start riding, you'll instinctively fix your attention on the machine and on an area about fifteen feet ahead of your front wheel. That's a bad way to ride, whatever two-wheeler you're on. As soon as you feel confident about controlling your bike, start riding with your attention fixed on the traffic and road surface conditions ahead, and learn to watch out for the opening of car doors, people or animals rushing into your path from between parked cars, holes, iron gratings, oil slicks, potholes, ruts, and broken glass. Concentrate far ahead of your front wheel, where all possible dangers await you!

Fast stop. Get used to making fast stops. Find out how your

Keeping a finger or two on the clutch is good insurance against unexpected emergencies. Note the right hand holding the throttle from underneath.

machine reacts to sudden slamming on of one brake and then both brakes. Stopping fast, without losing control, depends on the condition of your brake system, your overall weight, and the kind of road you're on. Stopping on concrete is different from stopping on sand, soft dirt, or a wet surface. Generally, for every ten miles of slow speed you'll need ten feet in which to stop. At 50 mph, you'll need about 130 feet of clear space! *Improve your riding skill to the degree where you hardly need to use the brakes!* Believe it or not, it's the style of the experts.

Set your mirrors right. Very often you won't have time to turn your head to see what's coming up behind you, and in those instances you'll have to depend on the mirrors. Set them so that you don't have to do more than flick your eyes to them to see what the conditions are

Set your mirrors so you can see what's behind you by merely shifting your eyes.

in the rear. If you have to crane your neck or change your body position to see the mirrors, it means you have not set them right.

Signaling turns. Use your left arm to signal left or right turns, as well as stops. Practice doing it, controlling the machine with your right hand, and as soon as you've made your signal, get your left hand back on the handlebar. The question "Was my signal seen?" may torment you in the beginning, and for this reason experienced riders add a look-see to the hand signal. In this way they're sure whether they're safe. All new motorcycles must have electric directional signals. Use them. And before changing lanes or making a turn, give a quick glance to play it safe. In many states the law requires that you use hand signals, even if you have electric directionals.

Leaning Your bike will change directions when you lean your body to one or the other side. By pressing your knee against the side of the tank (on motorcycles), you can force the machine into a curve. Never use the brakes nor slack off on the throttle when you're in a tight curve! This leaning practice comes in handy when you suddenly have to avoid something in front of you. Experienced riders use a unique method of snapping the machine over to get away from trouble. Practice it *carefully* by riding in a straight line, with both hands on the grips, and your body relaxed. Gently push the right grip forward. The machine will instantly lean to the right! If you push the left grip forward, you'll lean to the left. But do it carefully in the beginning because if you push too hard, you could end up in a slide. To study the technique, watch some high-speed racing around an oval track. In every turn to the left the front wheel of every motorcycle points to the right.

Rain and night. Both are dangerous conditions because car drivers claim that at such times they can't see a two-wheeler. Remember that your tires will not have the same traction on wet streets and roads as they do on dry surfaces. Especially when you lean! At night the reflections from various light sources tend to confuse car drivers and you. And remember that experienced riders avoid riding under these conditions whenever possible.

Your friends. Your friends will plead with you to take them for a ride and give them a thrill. Try your best to put them off until you're more experienced and can take them for a ride knowing you'll both be safe. If you feel you're ready to ride two up, then take the time to initiate your friend into the technique by taking a slow ride around the block. Your passenger should do nothing more than sit up straight (no leaning) and keep his or her weight forward. Don't scare your passenger with any fancy stuff, like a fast getaway or sharp turns, because there have been cases in which the frightened passenger jumped off and was badly hurt.

Other friends may ask you to join them in a group ride. Of course, this is fun, but some riders can create dangerous situations for the others. The first rule is not to ride bunched together—give each

Develop your confidence to lean into a curve without spilling. Sit with perfect posture and don't use the brakes when in a curve! This, of course, is not the limit of the lean for this BMW.

other space! On bicycles, string out so that you're one behind the other, and keep clear of the rider in front of you. On motorized machines, never ride more than two abreast in one lane, and keep a healthy distance between yourself and cars. Your big enemy in this kind of riding will be the temptation to outdo one of the other riders or to outdo a car!

Borrowing and lending. If you must borrow a machine from a friend or if you rent one from a dealer, do yourself a favor and immediately check out the action of the brakes. Too many people found out too late that the brakes were not taken care of. Play it safe. If the brakes don't feel right, bring it to your friend's (or the dealer's) attention, and get it fixed *before* going for a ride. And if you lend your machine to a friend, be sure to check it out after he or she returns it.

Imagine yourself in traffic. You're wearing your helmet and goggles or face and eye shield, and you're dressed properly. Everything on your machine is checked out, and you've gone through many hours of basic practice and have tried your hand at advanced techniques. You have studied the booklet for motorists and riders of two-wheelers, which is issued free by your local Department of Motor Vehicles, and you know the meaning of all traffic lights and signs. As for the many rules which you'll find in this booklet, don't look at them as mere rules but rather as traffic situations, and then use your imagination to place yourself in these situations.

For example, if you're riding up to an intersection which has no control signs and a car is approaching the same intersection from your right side, who has the right-of-way? The rule is: the car on your right. Now reverse the positions—you're on the right-of-way side, approaching the intersection, and you notice that the car driver is not going to obey the rule. He's ignoring you and heading through. Should you insist on showing him he's wrong and ride right into his path? Force him into a panic stop? Suppose you try it and he doesn't stop? He could be an indifferent, belligerent, or careless driver, and the point is that *he can hurt you* on your two-wheeler, whereas you can't hurt him. *Be smart, and don't tangle!* Such lack of courtesy deserves a smile from you because when that driver sees you smiling, he'll know you're the smart one.

Another example can be found at stoplights for two-way traffic. You're riding in the right-hand lane and intend to go straight ahead. A car facing you in its left lane is signaling it will turn left, meaning the car will cross your path when the light turns green. As the light turns green, you start forward, but the car speeds up and cuts right in front of you, causing you to brake hard to avoid an accident. The car speeds away. Who had the right-of-way? You, of course. The impatient driver of the car obviously does not obey rules. You'll have to resign yourself to such situations and be smart enough not to insist on your right-of-way. Or you can argue the point all the way to the hospital!

Look at other rules and traffic situations:

Keep right. Since you can't get a sudden burst of high speed out of a bicycle or moped, you can't beat the fast traffic or get out of harm's way. So ride your bike on the far-right side of the street, and as you ride along, look back every so often to see what's coming behind you. *In the distance of one block you should look back at least once,* and more often, if the traffic is heavy. You can use the side mirrors for checking, but the experts prefer to look.

Position yourself. Street and road lanes are marked with broken white lines so cars can position themselves. But a dark streak runs along the center of each lane, formed by oil drippings from cars. Any oily surface is slippery, so position yourself either to the left or right of these dangerous lines and with enough distance between yourself and the car in front. *Do not* make sudden lane changes! If you must change to another lane, check the rear before you swing out. If you must pass a car, make sure you have a clear lane in which to do it, and *don't try squeezing between cars in lanes* (it's illegal, anyway).

Guard your separation, front, back, and sides. Once you establish your position in the flow of traffic, guard it by not trailing too closely behind the car in front and not getting boxed in by the cars on the sides and behind you. You'll need space for stopping and for changing lanes. Cars can't get out of a tight spot as quickly as a two-wheeler, but even so, you need room in which to do it. Traffic may be flowing nicely one second, and in the next, all hell can break loose. Don't ride alongside cars in traffic—either let them go ahead, or get ahead of them yourself (if it's safe to do so). You're asking for sudden trouble if you ride too close to any car or smack behind a truck or bus when you have no way of seeing what's up ahead.

Blind curves and corners. Experience pays off. One day I was buzzing along the parkway in bright sunlight. My exit was coming up in another 500 feet. I checked the rear, which was clear, and changed lanes. I eased off a bit on the throttle as the road went downhill and into a left curve leading into the darkness of a short tunnel. I leaned into the curve and entered the tunnel. Then I almost slammed into a parked car with its hood up and the driver working under it. Somehow I managed to swerve aside, around the car, and again out into the sunlight. Had there been cars following me or alongside me, the incident might have turned out very differently. *NEVER speed into even a familiar blind curve!* The surprise of finding the unexpected there isn't worth it. And the same advice holds for corners, where you can suddenly come across spilled oil, potholes, rocks, and even people and animals. In the autumn, leaves covering road surfaces can be as dangerous as spilled oil.

Always be alert. Whenever traffic starts jamming up, it may be due to an accident up ahead, a bottleneck, or a traffic problem. That's when many drivers become impatient and start cutting in and out of lanes. You must be prepared for these eventualities. A train crossing sign visible in the distance says you'll be crossing tracks. The tracks may be deepset or raised and can be a problem for a speeding bike. Watch for parked cars when their lights are on (they may move suddenly) or when they're double-parked (doors could swing into your front wheel). If you're always on the alert, you at least have a chance to take evasive action!

Give way. Many vehicle operators undergo a change of personality as soon as they get behind the wheels of their cars. They become far too aggressive and will not yield an inch. They'd rather scrape fenders than let the other car get ahead of them. Little wonder for this attitude when one studies the car manufacturer's competitive promotional programs. Television, newspapers, and magazines show snarling panthers, roaring tigers, hissing mountain lions, and other related gimmicks which definitely influence drivers' attitudes. No two-wheeler that ever tangled with a four-wheeler came out the winner. So be smart, and give way to his arrogance.

Passing and crashing. Imagine a bicycle and moped rider following the traffic up a one-way avenue, breezing along effortlessly, keeping close to the parked cars on the right side and attentive to the traffic ahead of them. They approach some double-parked cars, check behind them, and swing into the left lane. At the next corner some cars are slowing down and turning to the right into the side street, and so both riders start passing. But one car suddenly swings out into their lane, and both riders try to speed up and pass the car. Neither the bicycle nor the moped has the necessary speed to pass, so they move over to the next lane.

Neither of them tried to stop because they feared the cars behind them. Now car brakes screech! Both riders had been paying attention to the traffic in front of them, but when they were forced to the left, they found themselves in the path of cars whose drivers were taking the traffic for granted. Pass on the left, but remember that you may have to speed up in order to complete your pass. A bicycle and a moped have no great passing ability in fast-moving traffic. On these machines you have the advantage of being able to wiggle through traffic, but do so at safe speeds and safe moments.

Scooters and motorcycles have more power, and are able to complete passes at high speeds. Practice and find out exactly how much passing power you have, and accept the fact that you can't push beyond that limit.

NEVER pass on a hill or in a curve. To make sure the car you're passing isn't going to surprise you, keep your eyes on his front wheel. It will tell you instantly what the driver is doing with the steering wheel.

The worst situation you can be in is to plan a right-hand turn at the

Whenever you pull away from a parking place, change lanes, or make turns, look before you open the throttle. Your eyes are more trustworthy than your mirrors.

next corner and have a car, bus, or truck on your left side. Don't be sure it's going to pass you and go straight ahead. It can cut you off, with bad results. This is a very common situation, not only at city street corners but also on highways where a turnoff can be made. So be on the alert, and don't place yourself alongside cars or other vehicles. If you can't avoid being boxed in, then give way to everybody, and prove you're the smart one.

Corner coming up. Every rider gets a thrill out of taking a corner at speed but is shocked when he or she finds something undesirable there. All corners and intersections, even those with stop and yield signs and traffic lights, are the places where unpleasant things can happen to you. It doesn't take much skill to speed around a blind corner or through an intersection. Anybody can do it, and if you admire that kind of riding, you ought to pray that your luck holds up when you try it.

A squeeze is no fun. A tight spot is one which makes you wish you were elsewhere because the crowding cars seem oblivious of what might happen to you. When you find yourself in a tight spot, stop and ask who put you there. You were either not paying attention to what was developing in the traffic ahead and suddenly found yourself surrounded, or else you saw the mess and went charging into it, defiantly or carelessly. By paying attention to what's developing in the traffic up ahead, you'll avoid getting into a tight squeeze, and you'll prove you're alert and conscientious.

Look before you lean. Soon enough you'll become bold, and traffic won't scare you anymore. You'll start speeding, cutting in and out of lanes, and believing that car drivers are constantly aware of your presence, easily guessing your next move. Then, one day, you'll cut into the next lane, and a surprised driver's car will cut you all up.

Accident statistics point out the fact that riders of two-wheelers meet up with accidents within their first six to eight months of riding. This is the time it takes to build up confidence and begin feeling that you're an expert in traffic and that nothing will happen to you.

Stop, and get ready. After you've come to a near or full stop, you'll need a technique that will move you out of there fast enough to keep up with the traffic. If you don't move out fast enough, you might create a problem for some impatient car driver, who could try to get around you and bump you into a spill.

Shift down, in steps, as you're coming to a stop, thus putting your machine into low gear. This does not apply to a moped because it has only one gear and a centrifugal clutch that will always start you up in that gear. When the light turns green, you're ready to move out faster than if you had to start up in a higher gear (on a bicycle) or start shifting down and looking for low (on a scooter or motorcycle). If the stop is a long one, use the neutral position with the clutch disengaged. Otherwise, you'll overheat the clutch plates. When the light turns green and the way is clear, pull away smoothly and steadily, shifting through the gears until you reach the one you need for the moving traffic.

The fast getaway. Many new riders love the thrill they experience when they open the throttle wide as soon as the light turns green. A burst of speed gives you a sense of power, and no money can buy that feeling. But if your two-wheeler could talk, it might say "Hey, buddy—this is okay on a racetrack but not here in a crowded street,

114 / Fun and Safety on Two Wheels

where my tank and fenders can get smashed." Want to prove how fast you are? Go out on a track and meet the real tough guys, who'll tell you, "Speeding and fast getaways in streets brand you a fool."

Smooth and steady are not easy. The toughest part of riding is to control completely your machine and your attitude. It takes a lot of willpower to move through traffic at a smooth pace, rather than zigzag or speed. Most professional competition riders are able to stand their machine up on its tail or nose, jump it over logs and brooks, almost climb the side of a mountain, but when they're in traffic, they know better than to show themselves up as fools. If you ever have the luck of tailing one of them through traffic, you'll notice the efficiency of every move. They hardly use their brakes, and you rarely hear them sound the horn! They just seem to glide with the flow of the traffic.

When you're more than one. Group riding can be a lot of fun for everybody. What it calls for is an experienced "leader" who is not

Be safe by keeping your separation, whether in empty suburban streets or in city traffic. Note the full and half (summer) helmet.

going to lead the pack to slaughter. The leader must think not only for himself but for every other rider in the group behind him. Riders who like to show off their ability to speed or swing from lane to lane don't really belong in a group that's out for an enjoyable ride, so be careful whom you're following!

Be bright. The law requires that the lights on motorized two-wheelers be switched *on* day and night when you're riding. You want others to see you, so obey the law and ride with your lights on. If you're riding a bicycle, be sure all your reflectors are clean and visible (at night you'll be safer if you outfit your bike with a set of lights).

Dress brightly, too. If your jacket is of dark material, you'll be wise to attach some inexpensive reflective tape across your back, waist, and sleeves. There have been too many accidents in which the car driver complained, "I never saw him until I was right on top of him."

The simplest rules of safety are to *watch the road ahead of you* and *pay attention all the time!* Any kind of distraction can create a bad traffic situation for you, in merely a split second. Riding calls for all your concentration. Never take anything for granted because traffic changes from second to second.

Don't ride when you're overtired. My third accident on a motorcycle was due to personal fatigue. I actually fell asleep! The sound of the engine was smooth and soothing, and I found I could close my eyes for a few seconds at a time. When the highway curved to the left, it wasn't yet time for me to open my eyes. I rammed into a car, my engine caught fire, and I was very awake. I put out the fire with my gloves, dragged the bike off the road, and waved to concerned drivers that I was all right. They drove off, and I looked around for the car I had hit. My knee was badly hurt. I was angry at myself and wondering what the driver would say. But there was no car anywhere in sight; whoever I had hit had driven away fast. I later wondered if he might have been driving a stolen car.

As soon as you notice your attention lagging, your lids feeling heavy, your ears refusing to pick up sounds clearly, and your mind picturing a soft warm bed, that's the time to pull off the road. And if you've been drinking, or using any kinds of drugs, don't get on your two-wheeler!

Long-Distance Touring

6

After building up a lot of hours riding short and average distances, you'll start thinking about faraway places you'd like to visit, as a lone rider or with several others.

One of my friends enjoys his 10-speed bicycle on a 100-mile run each weekend. Another friend rode his motorcycle from New York to the Daytona motorcycle races, while another rode clear across the United States to visit the great national parks of the West. He rode across the flatlands, the desert, and the winding, climbing roads of the mountain country.

One man on his BMW actually traveled from Alaska all the way down to the tip of South America. Another rider started on a 50 cc Jawa in Europe and made it across Siberia! Not long ago a New York doctor and his wife completed a bicycle tour down to Brazil, traveling for two and a half years over the best and worst roads imaginable.

All of it is an adventure in the form of a challenge for both you and your machine. But riding long distances is not the same as riding forty or even one hundred miles locally. The difference is that you'll be in strange territory, on unfamiliar roads in foreign towns and cities. With long distances facing you, your thinking changes, too, and you must prepare yourself and your machine for the trip.

During a discussion of long-distance touring, Ron Hansen, sales manager at American Jawa Ltd., in New York, offered some valuable pointers for the new rider. Ron is an experienced rider of long standing, who believes in safety at all times.

"Sure," he said, "I'll talk about it, and I'll start by saying that too many new riders don't plan sufficiently when they decide to go on a long trip. The idea is to be safe and comfortable, yet too many people don't even consider the kind of weather they'll be hitting—actually the kind of weather that'll be hitting *them*.

"The first thing I would do is get some good detail maps of the areas I'll be going through. It's a much better idea to have a planned route than just to meander along. I'd also take a list of phone numbers of dealers who'll be able to help in case parts or repairs are needed. Such phone numbers can be lifesavers!

"I would check out every part of my bike—every bolt, wire, cable, and lever to make sure it's in the best possible shape. Your bike may run without a single problem for a whole year, and then, when you're away from home, something could suddenly go out of whack. You've got to take along the usual spare parts and tools—bulbs, plugs, fuses, chain links, and such. Also take a good rain suit and a compact first-aid kit. And don't forget a long nylon towrope (which won't take up any room if you wrap it around the luggage rack), just in case you have to be hauled to a repair shop. Some riders carry a spare tube, but you might want to just take a tube patching kit and a can of compressed air. Then you won't have to use the hand pump all day just to get twenty pounds of pressure into the tire.

"And while we're on tires, I would suggest a little practice which you'll never regret. Pretend that you have a flat, take off the wheel, use the tire irons to get the tube out, and then put it all back together again. Fixing a flat is neither fun nor easy, so you'd better know how it's done *before* you start off on a long trip. Also take along at least one can of oil for the engine. When you need it and there's none around, you'll think of yourself as a genius for having packed it in your saddlebag. Even if the oil pump on your two-stroker failed, you would not be stuck. Just add some oil to the gas tank, and keep going. But make sure everything you're carrying is evenly balanced on both sides of your bike; otherwise, you'll be wondering what's wrong with your machine.

"In different states the exhaust noise level requirements vary, so check this out with your dealer. Laws about wearing helmets vary, too, but I would play it safe and wear mine all the time. As far as the actual riding goes, keep in mind the fact that you're not familiar with the roads, especially the winding ones in the mountains. Even in flat country you could meet up with the shrubbery-concealed side roads from which some half-asleep driver may come shooting out. Toward dusk animals may be crossing your path when you least expect it. Always anticipate the worst! It'll keep you on the alert.

"Don't overestimate your endurance. Some riders can go eight hours and more without stopping, except to take on gas, but others can't. Don't force yourself to keep up a pace which is too much for you. Be smarter than your ego.

"One word about a possible accident. The rule is: *Don't hit head on.* Go into a slide. If you're on a heavy motorcycle, the chances are you won't tumble, so a slide should be your best bet. Try to stay with the bike as long as you can, because flying clear is not always safe."

I asked Ron how he felt, personally, about wearing a helmet.

"Are you kidding?" he exclaimed. "You never ride without one. I'm not talking only about long-distance trips but even short runs around the village or in the city. And wear gloves and good shoes, or boots. I'll tell you one thing, there are an awful lot of hurt riders who are wishing too late they'd been smarter and had dressed properly for that little run around the block."

One late winter afternoon I was riding on a parkway and keeping my attention fixed on the many patches of ice all along the concrete surface. The sun had melted the snow, and throughout the day these patches of ice were plain water; but when the sun went down, the water puddles became frozen ice slicks. Traffic was light, and I had no trouble zigzagging around these dangerous patches. Every time I approached a bridge I'd stand up on the pegs and cut at an angle so the iron grating wouldn't throw me off balance. I was doing all right, taking no chances. Then I came over a rise and down into a flat section again, and again I saw the ice patches all over the road. I also saw what looked like a brand-new motorcycle lying on its side, chained to the steel divider, with the handlebar twisted and the front wheel crumpled. Ice, like oil, can flip you faster than you can imagine! This unlucky rider hadn't noticed the danger in time and had gone down. Maybe he was returning home from a long trip. Maybe he was tired. Maybe he simply lacked experience. Well, I was nearing home, and I warned myself to stay cautious and alert because most accidents take place inside your own familiar territory.

WEATHER FACTORS

Riding long distances in wintertime is not a problem if you use common sense and dress properly. At normal speed, even on a bicycle, temperature drops in relation to how fast you're moving. For example, if the thermometer indicates 30 degrees F and you're going at only 20 mph, the wind-chill factor will be about 4 degrees. That's cold. Increase your speed to 40 mph and you'll be enveloped in air of minus 6 degrees F!

Wear some sort of face protection, unless your helmet has a built-in face shield. Thick, warm gloves, thermal underwear, warm socks, and solid boots are a must. In cold weather your reactions are slower, especially if you're on a long straight road with nothing to do but keep your eyes on the far horizon. Speed and cold can be a death trap! Pay attention to every second of your time as it whizzes past.

The same feeling of security will envelop you when riding in rainy weather. You'll find the best position on the seat, and after that you won't bother too much to check the traffic around you. As long as the road ahead is clear, you'll hate to turn your head. You'll have no problem if you keep to the straight line at a steady pace. But if an unexpected side road should suddenly feed some cars into your path, you might feel too settled in to do more than merely lean into the next lane—where a car driver may not react quickly enough to avoid you.

Excellent protection against rain and cold is provided by full shielding, as shown on this BMW—the ultimate machine for long-distance runs.

To keep your mind at ease during your tour, the instruments on this BMW tell how the engine is performing, whether or not the battery is being charged, which lights are on, and even the time.

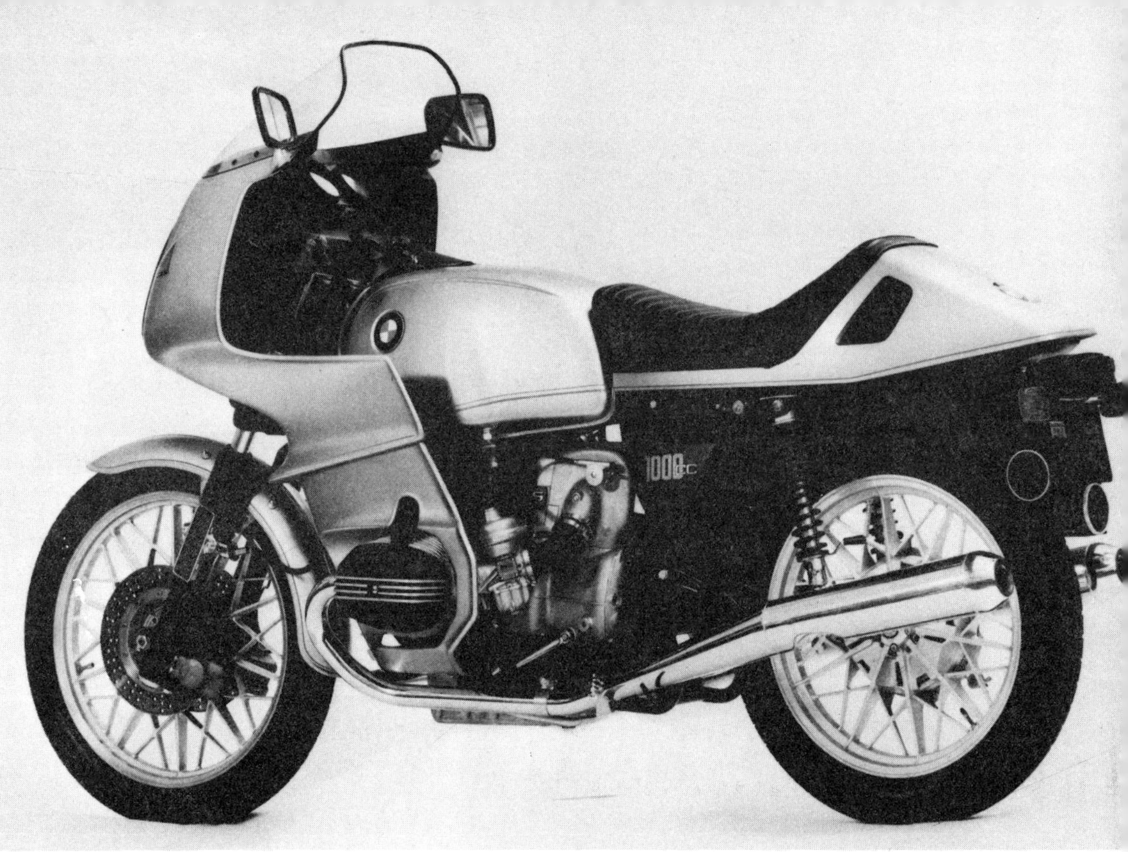
1000cc

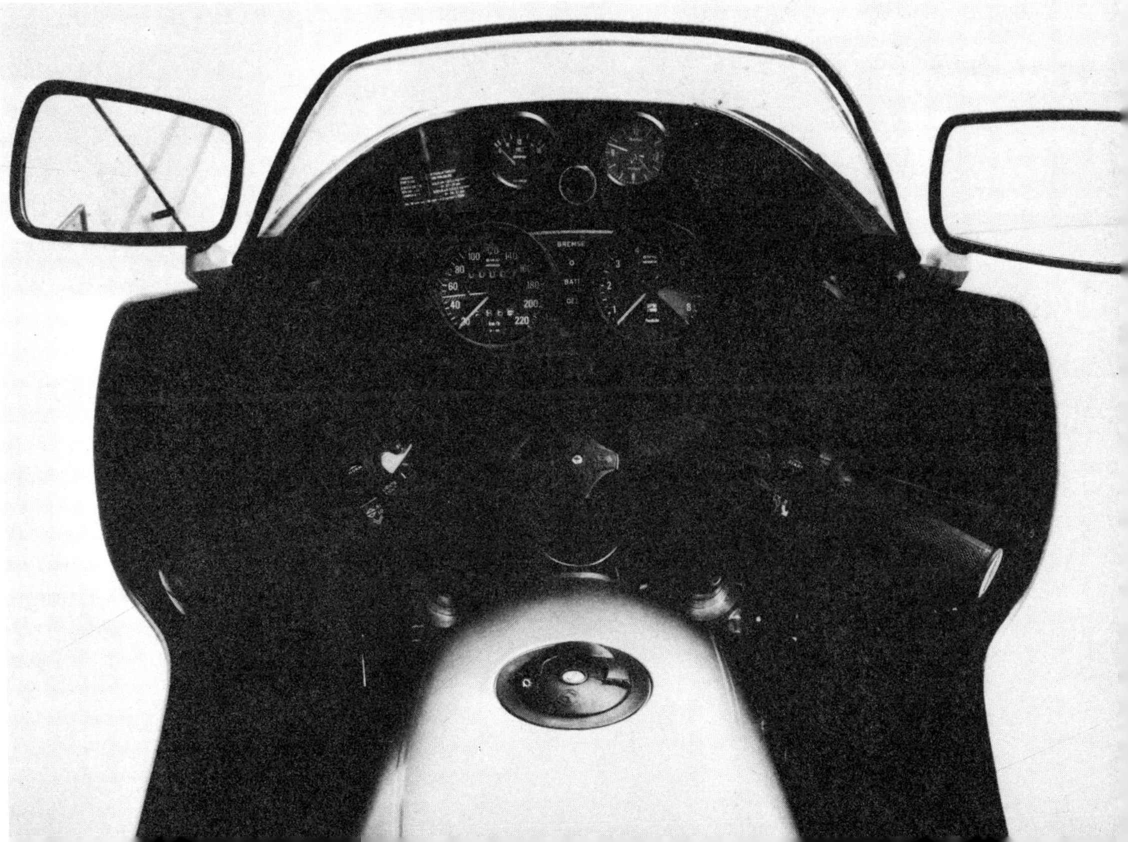
BREMSE

Fog is another dangerous weather condition. Riding at high speed through fog is especially perilous. Any time you can't see what's up ahead, slow down and prepare for evasive action. I was once on a strange country road in heavy fog when I had to crawl along in first gear, and at the crossroads I cursed myself for not having a compass because I couldn't even read the signs! Riding fast in fog guarantees one thing: You'll never see the tree, ditch, or car until you crash.

In warm weather don't wear loose-fitting clothing. A bee got inside the shirt of my friend, and he almost sailed down a mountain while trying to kill it. Concentrate on the machine first and the road ahead before you start attacking an insect inside your shirt or face shield.

ON THE HIGHWAYS

Through the efforts of various national safety programs, more and more bicycle pathways are being opened, and you should use these designated roads for your long-distance runs. If you want to see some interesting sights in a particular area, turn off onto the smaller local roads, where you can pause to rest, shoot pictures, and simply talk to people. Try to leave a good impression so that other riders who come by after you will be treated in a friendly way.

Passing through small towns may appear simple, but too often children and animals will dart out from nowhere and give you a hair-raising experience in evasive action. To the local residents the road is a peaceful place where they see no harm in crossing to the other side whenever the whim strikes them. Since they're not expecting you to come by, you had better expect them.

SUNDAY DRIVERS

The expression "Watch out for the Sunday driver" is not without reason. Originally the Sunday driver was one who took the car out on Sundays because he or she felt the roads would be empty, and therefore, lack of driving experience would not be noticed by others.

The Sunday driver is still with us but is now behind the wheel of a powerful car in fast-moving traffic. Sunday drivers usually talk with others inside the car and pay little attention to what's going on around them. They may have had a good time at a cookout or the beach. Train yourself to spot the Sunday drivers, and notice if they seem to be in animated conversation, oblivious of what might happen if even one car suddenly swerves out of line.

Don't be caught daydreaming!

HOW FAST PER SECOND?

If you're riding at 50 and a bad situation is developing a half mile ahead of you, you'll be there in no time at all. If you don't notice car stoplights flashing on, cars swerving or changing lanes, then you're really in for trouble. You can bring your bike to a fast panic stop, but can the driver behind you do it?

At high speed you have only a second to notice whether the road surface is strewn with sand, horse or cow dung, debris that's fallen off a truck, rocks, meandering children or chickens. Dogs love to rush out unexpectedly and greet you. Anything can happen in a split second. As a good rider you may be able to take evasive action, but only if you're alert for the unexpected.

Be on the alert when approaching toll booths, where the Sunday drivers like to come in fast, and without signaling, suddenly switch lanes for another booth.

OVERTAKING

During a long-distance tour you'll often overtake cars, buses, and trucks, and there won't be any danger involved if you do it alertly and sensibly. But you'll also meet up with the driver who can't afford to let anybody pass, and it happens on winding roads, uphill, and straight stretches. The overtaking often degenerates into a race and too often ends in a crash.

If you're smart, you won't let any fool lure you into a race. But if your attitude is the kind that must prove who's the better racer, then think in terms of a disaster. Have you ever seen what human flesh looks like after it has been shredded by concrete? And what do you imagine that kind of shredding feels like?

Don't tangle. And don't be a showoff.

Don't overtake any vehicle unless the highway ahead is clear for you. When it's safe, open up, and complete your run. Don't get up alongside someone and then dawdle because that kind of hesitation can create a problem for the other person as well as you. When you head downhill, it's best to stay in lane, without speeding up. And whenever you decide to make a pass, *always* check your mirrors first, or turn your head to look.

THE VALUE OF REST

Maybe you have greater endurance than four other riders, but that doesn't mean you can ride all day long without tiring. On a long trip, fatigue has a way of creeping up on you with very little warning. The hum of tires against the road creates a soothing sound inside your head, and you'll forget speed, distance, and the time it takes to stop. In your tired state, your muscles will relax to the point where you'll feel there's nothing to do but sit there, and you'll become indifferent, not caring what's happening.

On every road there are always interesting sights where it will pay to stop, stretch your muscles, and let your engine cool off. It can be an overlook, a rest area, or a grassy spot beside a stream. If you're with someone, he or she too may be feeling tired. Pull up somewhere and have a cup of coffee; then check out your bike. If you're a photography enthusiast, take the chance to use your wide-angle or telephoto lens.

Stopping to rest is smarter than pushing on just to show off how much you can do because you may not have the endurance you think you have. If anything happened to you or your passenger, your relatives and friends might say, "Well, he (or she) sure wasn't a good rider after all."

Of course, it's not all negative, for millions of car, bus, and truck drivers cover great distances daily without an accident. The same holds true for riders on their two-wheelers.

Rough Riding and Racing

7

Contrary to general opinion, caution and safety rules are not thrown to the wind with rough riding and racing. You'd be surprised how much attention is given to safety aspects by the American Motorcyclist Association, the main sanctioning and supervising body for the sport, in order to ensure a minimal risk.

Races attract thousands of spectators, most of whom are riders of two-wheelers who enjoy watching the competitors put their bikes through the paces. The riding is always a show of skill and daring. Watch a few motocross or trials events before you try it yourself. By watching and asking questions, you'll learn a lot. Write to the AMA for details about becoming a member, which you must be in order to compete, first as a *novice,* then graduating to the class of *amateur,* then *expert,* and finally *professional* rider.

Rough riding and racing are done on special machines. These machines are for off-road use and don't require registration (license plate). That means they usually have to be transported to the racing site by van, truck, or station wagon. Some dual-purpose bikes are ridden in off-road races and, since they're legally registered, can be ridden home on roads and streets.

I asked my old friend Don Whyte, who is still involved in competition riding, what advice he would give to someone who wanted to try it.

"The first thing I'd say," Don emphasized, "is to dress right so you'll be protected in case you fall, and then take it one step at a time.

Taking it step by step means getting in a lot of practice handling your bike in the woods and on rough ground because riding in competition is a lot different from riding in streets or speed-controlled roads. Take your bike to some deserted place where off-road bikes are allowed, like power-line access roads, an abandoned sandpit, or desert, and ride around to develop a feel for this kind of riding.

"But make it a rule never to ride alone. Team up with another rider just in case one of you ends up with a mechanical problem or gets hurt and can't ride back.

"You'll find that riding one kind of event appeals to some, and another kind of racing appeals to others. You'll have to find out for yourself what you like. For example, you might enjoy woods and trail riding, which doesn't have to be a race and for which almost any bike will do. You're out for some fun. You're not being pressed for time, so you can ride along the paths and over the rough ground, simply enjoying your machine in the great outdoors. But don't run around blindly, with no thought to the fact that others are using the same area, either on bikes or on foot. One rule when riding along the trails is to keep your speed down so you'll be able to stop within your visual range. At first, ride an easy trail to build up experience. Always be alert to what's ahead of you, and try to guess what could be around the next bush or bend. Don't run fast downhill when you're in heavily wooded areas. Don't be careless.

"Motorized two-wheelers are allowed in certain national parks, but the bikes must be fitted with approved spark arresters to prevent any chance of exhaust sparks starting a fire.

"Machines used for racing are designed for the job and are accordingly built with special features. The clearance from the bottom of the engine to the ground is high, the suspension must be capable of withstanding punishment from rough terrain and prevent loss of control, and the gearing and engine must provide the kind of torque best suited for the job. The usual tire tread for a motocross bike will be knobby, while that for a road racing machine will be a smoother design. One wheelbase would be short; the other, long.

You can cross streams, but be sure you have a way out on the other side. To keep the center of gravity low, this rider is up on the pegs.

"For best performance the weight of the machine is kept to the minimum, so whatever is not needed is discarded—such as headlamps, directional signals, horn, battery, and mirrors. Bikes with short wheelbases and high ground clearances are used for observed trials work in which the rider must demonstrate the utmost in skill. As he rides over rocks and logs and around various obstacles, a developed sense of balance and skill spells success or failure. Most of the riding is done on the pegs or footrests, and penalties are imposed if the rider's foot touches the ground or if the rider stops within a section or goes out of the boundary. This is not a speed race, but it takes a capable rider to go through it.

"On the other hand, the *enduro* is different in that the rider follows a route card, and the distance may be anything from six to over three hundred miles. The long ones are two-day events, and the shorter ones are set up in laps. Most of the run is over broken terrain, on rough roads and paths, and the riders usually keep to a time schedule, which is varied in order to make it more difficult. There are checkpoints along the way, but they're concealed to discourage 'cheating'—a rider loses two points for every minute arriving early and one point for every minute arriving late.

"A *motocross* and *scramble* are similar in that they're run over a rough track from a quarter mile to two miles long, with a lot of turns, hills, and jumps. A motocross may be a bit rougher, often producing a more interesting competition.

Here a motocross rider wears head and body protection, including leg guards.

A typical motocross bike of the 125cc class, this CZ sports knobby tires and a high clearance and uses transistorized ignition. It took second and third place in the 1976 World Championship Motocross Circuit.

"By way of advice, after riding in any event, you should check every part of your machine, fix whatever needs fixing, and wash off all the dirt and mud before you lubricate and oil the parts. Good riders don't just use a bike—they take care of it after each event so the bike'll take care of them in the next one."

The most grueling, yet the most prestigious competition is the world-famous International Six Days Trial, which is held in various countries. Riders qualify for these teams on the strength of their past performances in competition riding. During each day of the trial, rain or shine, the riders demonstrate their skill, courage, and endurance. Each carries spare parts and tools because all repairs must be made by the rider himself, without any help from outsiders. Refueling is permitted only at designated places. The coveted prize is the World Team Championship Trophy and, for best performance by a national team of four riders, the International Silver Vase.

To the newcomer on the scene all races may appear to be a whirling madhouse of two-wheelers. But that view is deceptive. Every official and every rider knows exactly what's going on and what to do. Flags of different colors are waved at the competitors to tell them of conditions ahead: when there's only one more lap to go, when something has happened on the track requiring an ambulance, etc. There's method in the apparent madness, and it's always under strict supervision. As in any sport, accidents happen and riders are hurt, but because every rider is fully aware of what might happen, each takes extra care to keep the odds down.

Former all-around racer Whitey Elligash from the New York Motorcyclist team consented to an interview, to stress the importance of safety. Whitey has plenty of experience behind him, having raced in motocross, enduro, short track, and various field meets. Like Don Whyte, he stressed the importance of dressing right and wearing an approved helmet.

I asked him what the first thing was that he did before a race. "Don't think I'm joking," he said, "but the first thing every rider should do is go through a warm-up. You know, loosening your muscles and joints, getting rid of any stiffness. All athletes do it before a game. You have to be in good shape for any race, and any beginner who thinks this is unnecessary will find out soon enough just how serious it is."

"And what about the bike?" I asked.

Whitey grinned. "Normally you do all the work yourself, unless you're a sponsored rider, in which case your team will have a topflight mechanic or two to take care of the machinery. I'm the kind of guy who likes to do his own work—that way I know what to expect."

"And if anything goes wrong, you have only yourself to blame?"

Totally different machines are used for the arduous International Six Days Trial (ISDT). Note the enclosed chain, headlight, and general simplicity of all the parts. At this writing, this Jawa type has been a thirteen-time World Trophy Winner, and took the Silver Vase sixteen times.

"Right. You sure get to know your bike."

"Tell me about the techniques used on the track. I know every rider has his own pet way of doing things. For instance, what's the best way to get away first when the flag drops?"

"Depends on the type of start. There's a rider's meeting before the race where you're told how things are going to be done. So you know whether they'll drop the flag or gate or use the hand-to-helmet start. The more races you're in, the more feeling you develop for this sort of thing. You try for the front because you don't want to be packed tight in the middle. Anything can happen when a bunch of machines are trying for first place, so you get out in front and try to stay there."

"Easy, isn't it?"

Whitey grinned. "Sure. Except everybody's trying to be first."

"Well, is there a best way of doing it?"

"It's a matter of concentration. Keep your body forward, and even use your feet to push off. You don't want the front wheel to come up, so keep your weight over the tank. Pour it on. Then just keep going."

"Then comes the first turn. What then?"

"The corners are the real test. There are no rules about it. If it's a left turn, all the smaller bikes will hug the left side. The big machines will have built up speed and will go to the outside. As the race progresses, every rider finds the best line or groove to use on the straight and around the corners. Keep away from ridges and rough sections, if you can. If it's a muddy track, don't put yourself right behind another guy because you'll be splattered from goggles to boot buckles. What you can do is watch which rider ahead of you is not bouncing as much as another, then follow him—he's in the right line!"

"What else?"

A shrug. "Just keep going, and pace yourself. You'll know whether you're riding slow or fast, and you'll also know when you're running *too* fast."

"In other words, don't take chances once you get out in front?"

"Well, if you can handle the speed on that track, do so. If you try to better it, you know you're putting everything you've got into one basket, and you might lose it. After all, you want to stay in the race. One spill will put you out."

"That's logical."

"Yes and no. One day you'll be hot, and you'll know you can do it; but on another day things will be different. Deep down you'll just know you haven't got what it takes. This happens sometimes, and riders have to accept it—even the best ones. The point is to ride and have fun; otherwise, you'd be doing something else instead of racing."

Another type of thrill-packed motorcycling event is the *high-speed road race*. Here the bikes compete in classes, everything from 50 cc on up to 750 cc, and the Open Class. All the famous makes can be seen whizzing past—Yamaha, Suzuki, Kawasaki, Harley-Davidson, Kreidler, Morbidelli, Husqvarna—all running to a time or lap limit. The famous Le Mans twenty-four-hour grind in France, for example, is run on the closed circuit regardless of weather, day and night, with two riders spelling each other on one machine. Road races in the United States are held in Riverside (California), Daytona (Florida), and at other tracks, with the experts coming from all over the world.

To get some good practical pointers to help the beginner understand how the pros do it, I spoke to Karel Bojer, who had successfully raced CZ 250 cc two-strokers and 350 cc and 500 cc four-strokers in many European road competitions. I asked how it's done from the fast start to improving your lap time to taking the straights, the bends and the hairpins.

"Everything," he said matter-of-factly, "begins with the machine being in perfect shape for the particular track and the rider being sure he can handle things. For a good start, like when you must run across the track to the machine and start it, you hope you'll have no trouble. If you get away with the first bunch, then you know you have a good chance to stay in front. After that you just keep going. It's all a matter of speed, but speed under control. If you lose control, like trying to go too fast through a bend, then you may spill. Once you spill you have the impossible job of catching up.

"Every second counts, so you have to keep your position and keep up your speed. You must know how far ahead of the bend to start braking. If you go in too fast, you'll go too wide and lose time. Going around lap after lap, you know what to look for, when to brake, when to shift down or up, and how much speed you can handle in the bends without spilling. When you pass the pits, your crew will signal to you, telling how closely you're being followed by the next rider. Then, when you come around on the next lap, you get the next signal telling how many seconds. If your distance is increased from the rider behind you, you know you're building up speed. If you can build up more speed and know how many laps are left, you know what your chances are of catching the leader and even passing him.

"One mistake in shifting, using the brakes, or leaning can be the difference between winning or losing a race. A spill is the worst thing for losing time and for getting hurt. You're going through the bends usually at fifty and down the straight at a hundred and thirty miles, and when you realize that you're going down, you know the machine will start spinning and turning. The best thing then is to let go of the bike and get clear. You don't want to be caught if the machine hits something with you in between.

"Luck often plays a big part in the outcome of any race. You may have a flat, a broken suspension or cable, or engine trouble. But of course, you always hope that nothing bad will happen and that you'll win."

If this appeals to you, check out your machine and start practicing. Personal experience in racing is the best teacher, and the only thing any book can do is point the way and explain some basic techniques.

So remember:

If you start to spill, keep your feet on the pegs as long as possible; then do your best to get clear of the bike.

Use your brakes *before* the curve, not when you're in it.

If the terrain is rough, get up on the pegs.

If you're running uphill, keep forward; if running downhill, keep back on the seat, and watch out how you use the brakes.

Too much speed may not get you through the rough sections.

In soft terrain like sand and mud, use a low gear and plenty of speed to prevent bogging down.

To control the machine, shift your body around to fit the circumstances.

THE BEGINNING OF GOOD RIDING

Neither the technical nor personal factors in riding two-wheelers safely are a problem. You can handle them. It's really nothing more than using common sense.

Continue using common sense and everything else you've learned.

Enjoy your bike and your riding.

And keep safe!

Index

Accessories, 29
Accidents, 11–13, 26, 55, 80, 82–84, 88, 90, 92–94, 125, 132
Acid, 66
Adhesion, 94
Adjustments, 31, 35, 39, 44, 46, 49, 50–52, 69
Air cooling, 64
Air filter, 56
Air leak, tire, 34
Air pump, 33
Alternator, 66
Amateur, 127
American Motorcyclist Association, 127
Animals, 119, 122, 123
Attitude, 10, 12, 26, 79–81, 83, 84, 87–91, 94, 97, 98, 100, 101, 103, 108–111, 113–115, 119, 124
Automatic centrifugal clutch, 22, 23, 25, 113
Automatic oil injection, 60, 62
Axles, 10, 32, 34, 46

Battery, 21, 23, 47, 64–66, 69, 75, 76, 129
   cables, 66
   cells, 66, 67
   charging system, 66
   ground, 66
Bead lubricant, 34
Bell, 19, 32, 47
Bell crank, 49
Benz, Karl, 20
Bicycle brake types, 35
   gear shifters, 49
Bicycles, 19
Bicycling, 86
"Bitter experience," 82
Blind curves, 110
BMW motorcycle, 117
Bojer, Karel, 135
Borrowing, 108
Brake, 10, 28, 84, 114
   arm, 35, 39, 42
   cable, 12, 35
   drum, 42, 43
   lever, 15, 16, 24, 35, 76, 99, 100
   pads, 35, 38, 42
   power, 90, 108, 136
   shoes, 35, 42, 43, 77
   system, 10, 104
Breaker points (ignition), 64, 68, 69
Buying a machine, 27, 28

Cables, 31, 35, 52, 136
Calculated risk, 89
Caliper brakes, 9, 24, 35, 43
Camshaft, 62
Carbon, 77
Carburetor, 55, 64, 68, 69, 71, 76, 77
CB radios, 29
Center of gravity, 103
Center stand, 100
Centrifugal clutch, 22, 23, 25, 113
Centrifugal force, 93
Chain, 24, 32, 39, 45, 46, 49, 76, 100
Check list, 53, 74, 131
Children, 122, 123
Choke, 70, 71, 77
Clearance, 128, 129
Clothing, 13, 87, 102, 108, 115, 118–120, 127, 132
Clutch, 21, 25, 26, 55, 59, 71, 101
   disengaged, 101, 113
   engaged, 101
   lever, 76, 102, 103
   plates, 100, 113
Coaster brake, 19, 23, 39
Coil ignition, 21, 64, 69
Cold engine, 64
Collision, 97
Combustion, 64
Competition, 13, 89, 114, 127, 131
Condensation, 76
Condenser, 64
Contact breaker, 64, 68
Contributing circumstances, 11
Control, 9, 11, 13, 16, 26, 29, 31, 35, 91, 97, 100, 103, 105, 114, 135, 136
Control signs, 11, 87, 90, 108
Controlled stop, 93
Controlling factors, 11, 90
Controlling force, 80
Cooling, 64, 65

Cornering, 102
Corners, 11, 110, 112, 134
Crankcase, 52, 60, 62, 64, 75–77
Crankshaft, 55, 62, 76
Crash, 13, 80, 97, 111, 123
Crashbars, 29
Cruising speed, 21
Current generating system, 66
Curves, 93, 100, 106, 136
Cylinder, 62, 64, 65, 77
CZ motorcycle, 135

Daimler, Gottlieb, 20
Dealers, 15, 27, 28, 118, 119
Death trap, 120
Decompression lever, 71
Defensive reactions, 79
Department of Motor Vehicles, 15, 23, 108
Derailleur, 28, 46, 49, 50–52, 100
Dipstick, oil, 52, 60
Dirt track, 88
Disc brake, 9, 24, 35, 39, 42, 43, 102
Displacement, engine cc, 62
Distance, 91
Distilled water, 66, 75
Distraction, 115
Downhill coasting (learning), 99–101
Drinking, 115
Drugs, 115

Efficiency, 114
Electrical connections, 66
   directional signals, 105
   power, 66
Electrolyte, 66, 75
Elligash, Whitey, 132
Endurance, 119, 131
Enduro, 129
Engine abuse, 64
   care, 75
   size (cc), 23, 62

Escape route, 83
Evaluation test reports, 28
Evasive action, 33, 110, 122, 123
Exhaust fumes, 23
   noise, 118
   sparks, 128
   system, 74
Experience, 26, 99, 103, 120, 128, 136
Experienced riders, 10, 12, 81, 97, 102, 106, 113, 127
Eye protection, 13

Fast stop, 86, 90, 97, 102, 103
Fast traffic, 109, 111
Fatigue, 115, 120, 124
Fear, 84, 86, 87
Feeling of security, 55, 83, 93, 120
Figure eights, 87, 102
Financial responsibility, 15
First-aid kit, 118
5-speed bicycle, 19, 45, 49
Flat tire, 118, 136
Flywheel dynamo, 64, 66, 67, 69
Fog, 122
Foot brake, 32, 35, 47, 100, 101
Foot rests, 101, 103, 129
Fouled sparkplug, 71, 76
Four-stroke engine, 20, 53, 62, 71
Frame, 19, 20
Friction nut, 52
Front fork, 28, 35, 44, 103
Fuel, 32, 52, 76
   bowl, 69
   filter, 56, 68, 76, 77
   line, 55, 76, 77
   mixture, 64, 70, 77
   valve, 53, 55, 58, 68, 71, 74, 76
Fuse, 47, 67, 69, 76

Gas cap vent hole, 68, 76

Gas tank, 52
Gaskets, 76, 77
Gas-oil mixture, 53, 56, 60, 62, 77
Gear shift lever, 100–102
Gearbox, 52, 53, 60, 62, 64
Gears, 21, 23, 26, 32, 45, 49, 55, 100–102, 113, 136
Generator, 66
Group riding, 106, 114
Guide pulley, derailleur, 46

Hand signals, 105
Handbrake, 24, 25, 32, 35, 42, 47, 101
Handlebar, 32, 35, 43, 44, 59, 99, 102
Handling techniques, 26
Harley-Davidson motorcycle, 134
Headlight, 19, 69, 129
Heat buildup, 65
Hedstrom, Oscar, 20
Helmet, 13, 87, 88, 119, 132
High speed, 13, 111, 134
Holding nut, 35, 38, 52
Horn, 19, 26, 32, 47, 69, 114, 129
Horsepower (hp), 23, 62
Hubs, 10
Husqvarna motorcycle, 135
Hydraulic fluid, 43

Ice, 119
Idle adjustment screw, 68, 100
Ignition, 21, 64, 69, 71, 74
Ignition switch, 68, 76
Indian motorcycle, 20
Inspecting, 31
International Silver Vase, 132
International Six Days Trial (ISDT), 131
Intersections, 87, 90, 91, 108, 112
Iron gratings, 103, 119

Jawa motorcycle, 117
Jawa Tatran scooter, 23

Kawasaki motorcycle, 134
Kickstarter, 70, 71
Kreidler motorcycle, 134

Lambretta scooter, 23
Lane changing, 91, 105, 109, 110, 123
Lean (when riding), 93, 94, 99, 100, 106, 113, 135
Lean mixture, carb, 70
Learning, 99
Lending, 108
License, 84
Lights, 32, 47, 100, 115
Liquid-cooled engines, 62, 64
Long-distance riding, 84, 117
"Lost control," 11, 94
Lubrication, 60, 62, 64, 65, 76, 131
Lugging, 65

Magneto, 21, 64, 66, 69
Maneuverability, 97
Manufacturers' promotional programs, 111
Maps, touring, 118
Mechanical failure, 11, 12
Mirrors, 32, 47, 104, 109, 124, 129
Momentum, 93, 94
Mopeds, 23
Morbidelli motorcycle, 135
Motocross, 13, 31, 88, 127, 128, 130
Motorcycles, 20

National Parks, 128
National Safety Programs, 122
Negative post, battery, 66
Neutral, gear position, 26, 101, 102, 113

New York Motorcyclist team, 132
Night riding, 106

Oil, 9, 10, 32, 46, 52, 60, 62, 64, 65, 76
 level, 53, 60
 level screw, 52, 60
 pump, 62, 118
Oily surface, riding on, 109, 110
Operating temperature, 62
Operations log, 74
Overheating, 77, 113
Overtaking, 123, 124
Over-tired, 115
Owner's handbook, 10, 14, 15, 33, 43, 46, 58, 62, 66, 69, 70, 74, 76, 77

Pace, 119, 134
Panic, 88, 93, 99
Panic stop, 26, 35, 87, 108, 123
Parked cars, 110, 111
Parts List, 15, 35
Passing, 111
Pegs, 101, 103, 119, 129, 136
Performance, 88, 97, 129
Periodic maintenance, 12
Personality, 110
Physics, 93, 94
Piston ring, 76, 77
Police, 22, 74, 81
Poor visibility, 11
Portholes, engines, 62, 103, 110
Positive post, battery, 66
Posture, 102
Power, 62, 101
Practice, riding, 86, 87, 95, 97–102, 105, 106, 108, 128, 136
Pressure, tire, 33
Professional, 127
Protection, 13

Psychologists, 81
Pushrod, 62

Quick-release hub, 34

Racing, 31, 62, 106, 123, 127, 128
Radar detectors, 29
Railroad tracks, 110
Rain, 106, 120
Rear hub, 38
Rear shock absorbers, 27
Reflections, 106
Reflective tires, 9, 19
Reflectors, 19, 32, 47, 115
Reflexes, 102
Regulations, 15, 108
Renting, machine, 108
Repair kits, 118
Research, 12
Reserve fuel, 53
Rest, 124
Rich mixture, 70
Riding requirements, 23
Riding techniques, 56, 113, 133, 136
Right-of-way, 81, 108, 109
Rights of others, 90
Road racing, 128
Road surface, 11, 93, 103, 104, 110, 119, 123
Rockers, valve, 62
Rough riding, 127

Safety equipment, 19
Scooters, 22
Scramble, 13, 130
Seat, 15, 32, 47
Seized engine, 58, 76
Self-starter, 21, 66
Separation, traffic, 109
Serial number, 18
Sharp turns, 87
Shifting, 9, 23, 26, 27, 135

Shifting pattern, 26, 101
Shock absorbers, 35
Signal, 91, 97, 105, 123
Silencers, 74
Single file, riding, 90
Single-speed bicycle, 19, 23, 38
Size, machine, 15
Skid, 93
Skill, 89, 97, 100, 104, 112, 127, 129, 131
Slide, 84, 94, 106, 119
Slowing down, 26
Snow, 119
Spare parts, 118, 131
Spark arresters, 128
Sparkplug, 64, 68, 69, 76
Sparkplug wires, 55
Speed, 21, 23, 91–94, 97, 99, 100, 101, 113–115, 120, 122–124, 135, 136
Spilling, 13, 29, 58, 97, 102, 113, 134–136
Sprockets, 45, 49, 65, 76, 100
"Squeezer" tool, 38
Starting an engine, 70
Statistics, 11, 113
Stem bolt, 43, 44
Stop blocks, derailleur, 50
Stop screws, derailleur, 50
Stoplights, 47, 89, 109, 123
Stopping, 84, 93, 97, 109, 128
Stopping an engine, 71, 74
Storage, long-term, 75
Sunday drivers, 122, 123
Survival, 80, 97, 99
Suspension system, 103, 128, 136
Suzuki motorcycle, 134
Swing arm, 35

Tachometer, 70
Taillight, 19

Temperature, 120
Temptation, 108
Tension, mental, physical, 18
Tension pulley, derailleur, 45
10-speed bicycle, 9, 19, 27, 45, 49, 117
Theft, 16–18
Theft insurance, 18
3-speed bicycle, 19, 27, 38, 49
Thrills, 88–90, 106, 112, 113, 134
Throttle, 10, 25, 26, 55, 68–71, 77, 93, 100, 101, 103, 106, 113
Tickler, carb flooding, 70, 71
Timing, 64
Tire pressure, 33
Tire traction, 84, 93, 106
Tires, 19, 28, 32, 33, 76, 84, 93, 94, 128
Tools, 32, 118, 131
Torque, 62, 128
Touring, 117
Towrope, 118
Traffic, 10, 11, 26, 81, 87, 90–92, 94, 95, 97, 108, 111, 113
  lights, 108, 109, 112
  pattern, 88, 92, 98
  rules, 81
  signs, 10, 11
  situations, 82, 83, 108
Trail riding, 128, 129
Trained mechanics, 27
Transistorized ignition, 64, 76
Transportation, 97, 101
Trials riding, 127
Trickle charger, battery, 66, 75
Trigger, shifting, 23, 49
Troubleshooting, 68, 76
Two-stroke engine, 21, 23, 53, 56, 62, 71, 77

Two-stroke engine oil, 62
Two-way traffic, 109
Tube, 34
  strip, 34
  valve, 32–34
Turns, 91, 97, 98, 105
Twistgrip, 23, 26, 49, 68, 70, 100, 103

Using both brakes, 100

Vent hole, gas cap, 68
Vespa scooter, 23
Vibration, 103
Voltage, 66
  regulator, 66, 67, 69

Warming up, 64, 71
Weather, 120, 122
Weaving, 99
Wedge, stem bolt, 44
Weight, 19, 20, 23, 33, 65, 93, 99, 104, 106, 129
Wet surface, 94, 104
Wheel, 32, 33
  hub, 10
  rim, 9, 32, 34, 38, 43, 75
  wobble, 10, 46
Wheelbase, 128, 129
Whyte, Don, 127, 132
Wind, 29, 93
Wind chill factor, 120
Windshields, 128
World Team Championship Trophy, 132

Yamaha motorcycle, 134

THE AUTHOR

Charles Yerkow is the author of three popular books from Putnam's: *Automobiles: How They Work; Motorcycles: How They Work;* and *Here Is Your Hobby: Motorcycling.* In addition to his enthusiasm for motorcycles and other two-wheelers, Mr. Yerkow's interests include aviation (he has a private pilot's license and has lectured on the subject at Queens College), and judo (he is a 4th-degree black belt of the Kodokan and his written several books on the sport). Mr. Yerkow lives in Beechhurst, New York, with his wife, Lila Perl, who is also an author of books for young adult readers.